The
Hairstyle
Hair Care &
Beauty Book

The
Hairstyle
Hair Care &
Beauty Book

by Linda Sonntag

CHARTWELL
BOOKS, INC.

A QUINTET BOOK

Published by Chartwell Books Inc.,
A Division of Book Sales Inc.,
110 Enterprise Avenue,
Secaucus, New Jersey 07094

ISBN 0-89009-832-8

This book was designed and produced by
Quintet Publishing Limited
32 Kingly Court, London W1

Designers Bobby Colgate-Stone and
Neil Strudwick, Mixed Media
Picture Researcher Vivian Adelman

Typeset in Great Britain by
Leaper and Gard, Bristol
Color Origination in Hong Kong by
Hong Kong Graphic Arts Limited
Printed in Hong Kong by Leefung-Asco
Printers Limited

The author gratefully acknowledges the help of
Jo Clair of Clairol Advisory Service in giving
technical assistance on hair and hair care in the
preparation of this book. All views expressed are,
however, those of the author.

Contents

Introduction

Today beauty is more than skin deep — it's feeling good as well as looking good. A healthy diet, with plenty of fresh fruit and vegetables and lots of mineral water to drink, regular exercise, fresh air and sleep will give you a sound foundation for your beauty routine.

Making the most of your looks need not cost you a fortune or be endlessly time-consuming. Once you have discovered the individual requirements of your own hair and skin type and acquired the simple skill of applying just the right amount of make-up, caring for your looks will become second nature. But there's always room to experiment with new ideas.

This book aims to help you keep your skin and hair in tip-top condition and achieve the image — with the right hairstyle and make-up — that *you* want to project.

Chapter 1

Cosmetics– A Compact History

Cosmetics have been used in the art of being beautiful by both women and men for thousands of years. The Gauls dyed their hair red with goat's grease and beech ashes; the Anglo-Saxons went punk with green, orange and blue locks; while the Greeks opted for a more sophisticated look, streaking their hair with gold and silver powders. It was the Greeks who were also responsible for popularising the use of white lead. Powdered on the face, it made a person pale and interesting and covered the ravages of disease, but it eventually ruined the complexion completely — and continued to wreak havoc with women's faces well into the nineteenth century.

It was the Egyptians who first manufactured cosmetics on a large scale — and the preparations they used are surprisingly similar to today's. The Egyptian lady's eyes were ringed with dusky kohl and her lids shaded turquoise with a powder made from green copper and lead ore. Lips and cheeks were rouged with powdered red clay and the palms of the hands, the soles of the feet and finger- and toe-nails were given a rosy glow with an application of henna. Hygiene was a priority. Cleopatra bathed in asses' milk, which softened and conditioned her skin, and high-born men and women anointed their bodies with spiced and scented oils. Both sexes shaved their heads and wore intricately styled and elaborately ornamented wigs.

The excavation of ancient Egyptian tombs has revealed beautifully worked cosmetic pots — some still containing traces of ointment; tiny spoons, palettes, bowls and pestles used for measuring, mixing and grinding coloured powders; ornamented containers for kohl sticks, bejewelled perfume jars, metal mirrors and hairdressing tools such as combs and curling tongs.

In ancient Rome powerful bleaches and hair dyes were used so rigorously that baldness often resulted. But before the society lady resorted to a

Queen Nefertiti was renowned for her natural beauty, which she enhanced with kohl eyeliner and clay lip powder

Queen Elizabeth I of England preferred no colouring and contrived a white complexion with pastes and powders

The seventeenth and eighteenth centuries saw even more absurd efforts being made to counter the effects of ageing. A poor diet, a dissipated lifestyle and the use of white lead meant that the faces of the upper classes were disfigured with pimples and pock marks that no cosmetics could conceal. A vogue for patches sprang up. These were cut from black or red silk in decorative shapes and glued to the offending spot.

In Edwardian times elaborate hairstyles were the rage and women painted their eyes, cheeks and lips in emulation of beautiful Queen Alexandra

wig, she often tried to remedy her problem with pungent conditioners made from dung. While her hair was falling out she was busy ruining her skin by caking her face and neck, shoulders and arms with white lead.

The bloodless look was brought into vogue in England by Queen Elizabeth I, who used white lead and masks of egg white, ground alabaster and clay to intensify her natural pallor. A pale skin indicated refinement, as opposed to the ruddy complexion of the peasantry, and every precaution was taken to avoid exposure to the sun. Elaborate and padded clothes were the order of the day — and even the hair was padded or turned over wire frames to create the illusion of extra volume. Clothes and headdresses were so cumbersome and difficult to remove, let alone to clean, that personal hygiene reached a low ebb and powerful scents, such as civet and musk, were used to try and disguise unpleasant body odours. As Elizabeth aged, she hid her thinning locks under intricately dressed wigs, and painted blue veins on her whitened forehead to create the impression of a youthfully translucent skin.

Another precarious beauty aid was the false eyebrow. This was made from mouse skin and worn enthusiastically by both sexes, though the device must have given rise to some embarrassing moments. Plumpers were an equally uncomfortable innovation. These were pads worn inside the mouth to plump out cheeks sunken by the removal of rotten teeth. They restricted conversation to an incoherent minimum. More serious harm was done to the eyes, which were treated with drops of belladonna — deadly nightshade — to dilate the pupils and simulate sexual arousal. Overuse of belladonna irrevocably damaged the eyesight.

Meanwhile, on top of the head, the hair of the fashion-conscious was twisted through a labyrinthine superstructure of frames, pads and hairpieces and glued in place with lard. The construction of these edifices caused hours of discomfort and so they were left standing for as long as they held together. Thus they became a haven for lice, cock-

As women became more emancipated, hair was styled to frame the face and attention was drawn to the eyes and mouth

roaches and fleas, and it was not uncommon to find a mouse nesting in your hairdo.

The beaux and belles of the Regency period could not cap these mad excesses. Instead they changed the trend and chose a fresher, more natural look. Make-up became more discreet and less damaging to the skin, and powdered wigs fell out of fashion, making way for softer styles. Cleanliness

became easier to achieve, and more desirable. In the Victorian era, personal hygiene became a positive obsession and home-made herbal preparations enjoyed a tremendous vogue. Make-up was frowned upon as being indicative of an immoral character, and cosmetics had to be applied discreetly and in secret.

Victoria's daughter-in-law, Queen Alexandra, revived the

In the late 50s women enjoyed looking sensual and feminine. The archetypal beauty was Marilyn Monroe, with her short bleached hair softly waved and her deep red lips covered with lashings of lip gloss

The boyish fashions of the late 60s were epitomised by Twiggy, with her close cropped hair and pale lips. Attention is focussed on the eyes with their exaggeratedly long lashes

popularity of painted faces, and women were soon copying the exaggerated looks of the stars of music hall and vaudeville. With the advent of the cinema, a chalky complexion, rouged cheeks, dark eyelids, bright bow-shaped lips and, later, platinum blonde hair became all the rage. The 1914-18 war liberated women somewhat from the glamour-queen stereotype, as did World War II. Women who worked in factories cropped their hair for safety and convenience, and were not embarrassed if they were seen applying their make-up in public.

Lipstick was the most important item in any woman's cosmetic bag — and no one felt dressed without bright red lips until the 1960s, when lips paled almost to insignificance beneath hugely emphasised eyes. Black eyeliner, often three layers of it, underlining upper and lower lashes and marking the crease of the eyelid, was supported by hard, brightly coloured eyeshadow and enormously long false lashes. The lower lashes were often painted onto the skin with eyeliner. So as not to detract from this show, lips were painted out in the most pastel of sugar pinks — or even in white.

In the 1970s the hippie movement encouraged a back-to-nature trend and many women threw away their make-up and let their hair grow long and untamed. But even the most beautiful woman benefits from having her looks enhanced and her hair styled to suit her face, and the results were mostly pale and *un*interesting.

With the advent of the 1980s came a revival of enthusiasm for natural beauty products, such as lanolin, oatmeal, witch-hazel and herbs. Cucumber and avocado came to be prized amongst vegetables, and lemon and strawberries amongst fruit.

Looking and feeling good, with glossy, well cut hair and a clear, fresh skin is a tremendous boost to any woman's ego. This book will tell you how to make the best of your natural resources, and how skin care, hair care and make-up can achieve stunning results and keep you looking younger — longer.

A stylish sculpted crop from the late 70s, when new importance was placed on a clean line and hair in superb condition

HAIR BY TREVOR SORBIE

Chapter 2

Hair and Skin-The Facts

For skin and hair to be beautiful, they must be clean and healthy. Glossy hair and a glowing complexion can be achieved by anyone who understands the requirements of her own skin and hair types, who treats them gently and with care. They need to be nourished from the outside with the right creams and conditioners — and from the inside with a healthy diet.

Skin

Skin is a living organ that covers the whole body. It is the body's largest organ, measuring about 1.5 square metres. Its thickness varies from 0.05mm on the eyelids, where it is at its most delicate and translucent, to 0.6mm on the soles of the feet, where it is at its toughest. With the exception of the palms of the hands and the soles of the feet, the skin is covered with hair follicles.

The skin's function is to protect the body, to help regulate body temperature by perspiring, and to excrete waste products such as water and salt.

Skin consists of three layers — the outer layer, the epidermis; the dermis, which is full of glands and blood vessels; and the hypoderm, a fatty tissue that nourishes the dermis and acts as a cushion between it and the muscles beneath. The epidermis has no blood vessels, and this means that it will heal without a trace. Its surface cells are flat and horny — they are, in fact, dead, and being constantly shed. They

flake off with friction from clothes or bed sheets, or get washed away in the bath. Other cells from beneath replace them. If the skin is exposed without a protective cream to harsh conditions, such as blistering sun, biting wind or stinging cold, cells will be shed at a faster rate and the skin will become red and raw.

The dermis, being full of blood vessels, scars when it is damaged. It is responsible for the changes of colour that signal our moods. Emotions trigger off a set of physical and chemical reactions in the body. The blood vessels in the dermis dilate and we flush with anger, embarrassment or pleasure; they shrink and we blanch with fear or nausea. The sebaceous glands in the dermis secrete sebum — the skin's natural moisturiser. A perfectly balanced skin occurs when sebum is secreted in exactly the right proportion. The skin will then be soft, supple and fine-textured. It will be smooth and blemish-free, rose-tinted and translucent. A perfect complexion is a rare phenomenon, but fortunately a lot can be done to improve an imperfect one. Underactive sebaceous glands cause dry skin, and overactive ones, oily skin.

Hormones circulating in the bloodstream stimulate the pigment cells to produce colour. They also control the production of sweat and sebum. This explains the changes in the skin's appearance at different times in the menstrual cycle and during and after pregnancy. Hormonal imbalance, which is inevitable at the onset of puberty, can cause enlarged pores — a problem that often results in black-heads and acne.

The dermis also contains the nerves, which are dense in some areas of the body and sparse in others. The concentration of nerves can also vary from person to person, making some people more sensitive to tickling in, say, the ribs, and others to tickling in the neck or on the soles of the feet.

Skin, our contact with the

elements, is bound to show the effects of use and abuse, and the process of ageing. Skin can age prematurely because of illness, an unhealthy diet, heavy smoking or drinking, or overexposure to heat, cold or a humid climate. But if you are to keep a clear, smooth and young skin, you should start caring for it properly, with a twice-daily cleansing, toning and moisturising routine, as early as possible.

There is no doubt that skin is at its best while young and fresh. A healthy child enjoys a complexion of peachy softness and creamy texture, but youth is not always a guarantee of problem-free skin. Even babies can suffer from rashes and allergies.

Puberty is often a bad time for the skin. The hormonal upheaval in the body is conducive to acne and also stimulates the follicles into producing unwanted facial hair. This will usually fall out as the body settles down, but it can be disguised by bleaching.

During the early 20s your skin should look at its best. This is the time to watch out for allergies that could continue into maturity, for the effects of different brands of make-up, and of drugs such as the Pill,

detergents, chemicals and insecticides. In the late 20s and early 30s the skin will begin to lose the bloom of youth. You should watch out for a tendency to dryness and change to a richer moisturiser. Anyone who has always had a dry skin will notice fine lines appearing as the 30s advance — dry skins tend to age more quickly than oily ones. Tiny broken blood vessels may appear round the nose or on the cheeks. These can be disguised by skilful make-up.

As hormone production slows down in the 40s, the skin begins to lose its tone, strength and elasticity. The protein fibres in the dermis sag, leaving the epidermis undernourished. Wrinkles and bags form, and the skin dries, becoming loose and flabby. In the 50s the skin often develops brown spots as the colouring agent, or pigment, moves. This, too, is the time to watch out for skin cancer. There are four basic types of this disease, which is often caused by over-exposure to the sun. It manifests itself in brown or red blotches on the face and is usually responsive to treatment, although some scarring may remain. The most serious kind is malignant melanoma.

A brown, black or blue blotch appears on the skin and indicates the presence of a growth. This must be removed to prevent spreading.

Many women, during and after the menopause, experiment with hormone creams for wrinkles around the eyes and throat. These are said to plump out the flesh beneath the wrinkles and indeed they do seem to work, though the effects may last only a couple of hours. Hormone creams are very expensive, and if you do decide to try them, you may find it worth alternating daily between the hormone cream and your usual moisturiser to spread the cost. Or you can use the hormone cream for three-month periods — this way you may be more aware of its benefits.

The enlarged cross section shows in simplified form some of the components that make up the largest organ in the body — your skin. Healthy skin looks good if it is well moisturised, and most of the oils needed to keep the skin supple are produced naturally

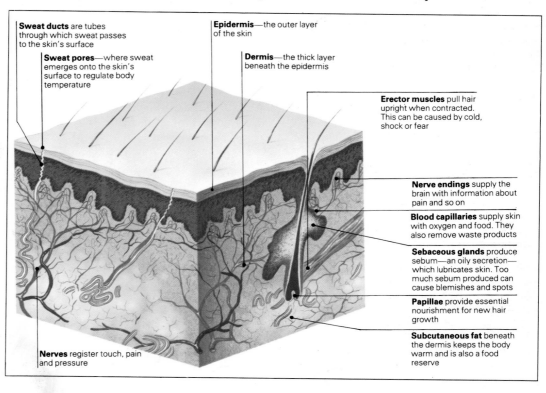

Sweat ducts are tubes through which sweat passes to the skin's surface

Sweat pores—where sweat emerges onto the skin's surface to regulate body temperature

Epidermis—the outer layer of the skin

Dermis—the thick layer beneath the epidermis

Erector muscles pull hair upright when contracted. This can be caused by cold, shock or fear

Nerve endings supply the brain with information about pain and so on

Blood capillaries supply skin with oxygen and food. They also remove waste products

Sebaceous glands produce sebum—an oily secretion—which lubricates skin. Too much sebum produced can cause blemishes and spots

Papillae provide essential nourishment for new hair growth

Subcutaneous fat beneath the dermis keeps the body warm and is also a food reserve

Nerves register touch, pain and pressure

Hair

Your hair is a valuable natural fibre and to get it looking at its best you should treat it with as much care as you would silk or wool. Fortunately, hair is very resilient. It is as strong as aluminium, and an average single hair can withstand a pull of 200g, which would snap most textile fibres. A healthy hair can be stretched by one fifth its normal length before breaking. If your hair is in poor condition because of neglect, or if it has been subjected to harsh treatment, all is not lost. With care and attention you will be able to restore its bounce and glossy sheen.

Hair grows all over the body except on the palms of the hands and the soles of the feet. The average adult scalp sprouts about 100,000 hairs; it is hair colour that determines the quantity. Redheads have thick hair, but the smallest number of strands. Next come brunettes. Blondes, who have the finest hair, have the greatest number of strands — up to 150,000. Black hair is the coarsest of all — the diameter of one black hair can be three times that of a blonde hair.

A single hair lives and grows for between two and six years — and in some cases, up to 20 — though, technically speaking, the hair shaft is dead matter, and only the root is alive. The shaft emerges from the papilla, a nodule at the base of the hair follicle below the surface of the skin. Hair growth cannot be stopped if a hair is pulled out by the root, because the papilla will eventually produce a new hair. The shape of the follicle determines the shape of the hair. A round follicle will produce straight hair that will usually grow long; an oval follicle produces wavy, medium-length hair, and a kidney-shaped follicle, most often found in black-skinned people, produces hair that is woolly and wiry and usually short.

Hair is 97 per cent protein and 3 per cent moisture, so the importance of protein in the diet for healthy hair is obvious. Each hair is made up of three layers. The inner core or medulla is the 'marrow' of the hair and is soft and spongy. It can deteriorate in old age and be damaged by drugs and chemicals. In some cases it is missing altogether and the hair becomes thin and brittle. The medulla is surrounded by the cortex, which is composed of long, thin, fibrous cells that give the hair its elasticity. The cortex contains the pigment that gives the hair its natural colour.

Pigments are red, yellow and black, and a mixture of these over the entire head gives the hair its individual shade. If no pigment is present, the hair is white. There is no such thing as grey hair — this is an illusion caused by white hairs appearing amongst hairs of the original colour. The cortex is the part of the hair that responds to chemicals intended to permanently curl, straighten or colour it.

The outer layer, the cuticle, is formed of hard scales of keratin, a protein, that overlaps like tiles on a roof. The cuticle protects the hair shaft. When the scales are lying smoothly, they reflect the light and give the hair its shine; they also trap the oil that gives the hair its lustre. This oil, or sebum, the hair's natural conditioner, is produced by the sebaceous gland attached to the hair follicle. The hair is lubricated as more sebum is produced, but the ends of longer hair will never be reached — you will need to

Hair by Clairol

HAIR BY CLAIROL

use a conditioner and trim off split ends. Lubrication is also stimulated by the tiny muscles around the follicle. It is these muscles that are responsible for the hair 'standing on end' through cold or fear.

Hair begins to grow before birth, but it is a myth that it continues to grow after death. It is the last part of the body to decay. Everyone loses, on average, 50 hairs a day, and these are replaced, except in the case of thinning hair, by new growth. Hair grows at the rate of about 1cm per month. Strangely, it grows faster in summer than in winter, and faster during the day than at night. Women's hair grows faster than men's. Cutting hair does not accelerate growth, though shaving hair under the arms and on the legs may make it appear coarser because it then grows with a blunted end.

A baby may be born with very little hair, or with a lot. Its hair may fall out in the first weeks of life and then begin to grow again, and its hair type and colour may change. But by the time a child is about three, it will have settled down with the hair it will grow up with. A baby's head should always be washed along with the rest of its body at bath time. Avoid putting pressure on the soft crown of the head, but wash it gently to prevent the formation of a scaly condition called cradle cap. If this does appear, it can be treated with cotton wool soaked in warm oil to soften it before washing in the normal way.

Children's hair is as easily affected by diet as adults' hair is. Encourage your child to eat fresh fruit and vegetables, and to avoid sweet and greasy foods.

Hormonal changes in the body and an active lifestyle are often the cause of lank and greasy hair in teenagers. A diet that is low in fats, sugar and carbohydrates should be encouraged. Adolescents should also be encouraged to wash their hair as often as they want — even twice a day won't harm the hair, as long as a gentle shampoo is used and the hair is allowed to dry naturally. Conditioner need be applied only at the ends of long hair.

Dandruff is another problem that can arise during the teens. If frequent and thorough shampooing with a mild shampoo does not help, try a medicated brand. Dandruff in the teens is sometimes caused by dirt, grease and shampoo being left behind on the scalp. Wash and rinse the scalp carefully. If the problem persists, consult a trichologist.

Split ends should be trimmed off. These can be exacerbated by the excessive use of hairdriers and heated styling equipment.

During the 20s, when life gets into full swing, it may be tempting to take advantage of the fact that your hair is enjoying maximum health and expect it to bounce back of its own accord every time you perm or colour it, or every time you expose it to holiday sun or the chlorine of a swimming pool. Use a nourishing conditioner on damaged hair or rub in warm olive oil or a wax cream, then wrap your head in plastic film, tie it in a scarf and leave it for as long as you can — overnight if possible. Protect your hair from the sun under a hat or scarf. If you go swimming, always rinse salt water or chlorine out of your hair straight away, then shampoo and condition. A conditioning gel is an excellent idea for keen swimmers and sunbathers. Apply it generously to your hair before you go to the beach to achieve a wet look that will be quite in place and will protect your hair all day.

Pregnancy affects the hair in different ways — sometimes it makes it more lustrous, but other women are less fortunate and find themselves losing quantities of hair. Some mothers-to-be find that their perm loses its bounce. Nothing can be done about this, but a healthy diet will ensure that the hair regains its former condition as soon as possible after the birth.

A common problem in the 30s is a tendency to dry and brittle hair. This is sometimes the result of years of perming and colouring, but it is more likely due to stress or a bad diet. A certain amount of drying up is inevitable as the body's functions begin to slow down and the production of sebum is reduced. This is the time, too, when most people discover their first grey hairs. These are actually white hairs, which look grey when mingled in with hairs of your natural colour. Many women in their 40s decide to disguise their grey hairs with a specially formulated rinse. At this age you should use a rich shampoo and pay special attention to conditioning — a wax or oil treatment once a week will bring back the life into your hair. Henna treatments restore the shine to dull hair, but use one without a colorant on grey or white hair, or you may be dazzled by the result.

During the menopause, hormonal imbalance and the emotional stress that often goes along with it can cause significant hair loss, while facial hair may coarsen or grow darker. Many women find hormone replacement therapy (HRT) keeps their hair in good condition and stops it falling out. At the same time it benefits the skin, slowing down the deepening of wrinkles. It has other advantages, in that it helps the flesh to stay firmer longer and the spine to stay erect, and a continued dose of oestrogen cuts down the risk of a heart attack.

Whether to opt for HRT or not is a decision for each woman to make in consultation with her doctor. If you decide against it, you should be able to avoid distressing hair loss by keeping to a healthy diet, taking frequent exercise to stimulate the circulation, keeping the scalp scrupulously clean and using nourishing conditioners.

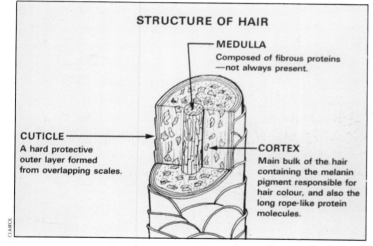

STRUCTURE OF HAIR

MEDULLA
Composed of fibrous proteins —not always present.

CUTICLE
A hard protective outer layer formed from overlapping scales.

CORTEX
Main bulk of the hair containing the melanin pigment responsible for hair colour, and also the long rope-like protein molecules.

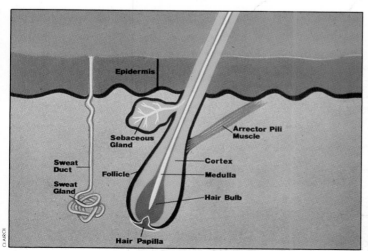

Epidermis

Sebaceous Gland

Arrector Pili Muscle

Sweat Duct

Follicle

Cortex

Medulla

Sweat Gland

Hair Bulb

Hair Papilla

Chapter 3

Skin Care

Your Body

Personal hygiene is the most important factor in your beauty routine and a bath or shower every day — or more than once a day in hot sticky weather — is the first step to freshness. Baths are most relaxing if they are taken warm, not hot, with a little fragrant bath gel or foam. You can make your own herbal bath by tying a bunch of herbs and sweet-smelling wild flowers in a muslin bag and hanging it from a loop beneath the hot tap while the water is running. In hot weather a tepid bath will cool you down, or a cold shower, with the water jet on full, will tone your muscles and leave you tingling. After your bath, rub body lotion into your skin and use a deodorant, unless you're going to bed.

Your skin is a living organ and its condition will reflect your lifestyle, your diet and exposure to the elements

Your Face

Whatever your skin type or age, the vital routine for every face is the same. You will need a cleanser, a toner and a moisturiser. You will also need an eye make-up remover. From time to time you can refresh your skin with different masks, and as you get into your 30s you'd be well advised to invest in eye and throat creams as well as a nourishing night cream.

Before you stock your dressing table with these essential products, you will need to discover your skin type. The perfect complexion is supple and translucent, moist without being oily. Most people have skins that are dry, oily, or a combination of both. An oily skin will leave a transparent mark on a piece of tissue paper pressed against it; a dry skin will tend to flake. Many women have an oily forehead, nose and chin, and dry skin on their cheeks. Choose the products that are suited to your skin type.

Sellotape may also be used to test for oiliness

The way you apply your cleanser, toner and moisturiser is important. Facial skin, especially round the eyes and on the neck, is very delicate, and must be treated with care. The muscles beneath, too, should be encouraged to stay elastic and mobile, as sagging causes wrinkles. Don't scrub at your face — broken veins as well as wrinkles will be the result.

- Use upward-sweeping strokes on your neck.
- Massage up from the chin and out past the corners of the mouth to the cheeks.
- Stroke outwards and upwards across the cheeks towards the side of your face.
- Work around your eyes from the inside to the outer corner both above and below the eye.
- Begin at the centre of your forehead and stroke upwards and outwards to the hairline.
- Stroke down the length of your nose and out toward the cheeks.

If you prefer soap and water to a cleanser, choose a mild unperfumed soap and keep it away from your eyes. Use lukewarm water, rinse thoroughly and finish with a splash of cold water to close the pores.

For an oily skin, choose a milk or lotion. A cream cleanser is best suited to a dry or combination skin. Remove all traces of soap or cleanser after use

The next step is toning. A toner will remove all traces of grease from the skin, refresh it and close the pores. Make sure you choose an alcohol-free toner if you have a sensitive skin.

Follow with your moisturiser to nourish and protect your skin. A heavier night cream should be used before you go to bed, especially on drier skins.

A face mask is a very good tonic for a tired skin. It will remove dirt and flakes of dead surface skin and leave your

MOISTURISING To prevent the skin from losing vital oils, use a moisturiser after you have completed your cleansing routine

Baby lotion for combined moisturizing and cleansing

Light greaseless moisturizer

Moisturizing To prevent an undue loss of water from your face, use a moisturizer regularly after you have completed your cleansing routine.

Dry skin cream for delicate complexions

Salve to prevent lips chapping

Thick moisturizing cream for dry skin

Light moisturizing cream

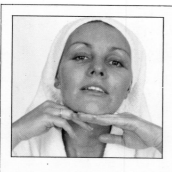  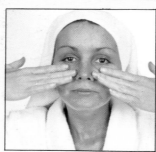 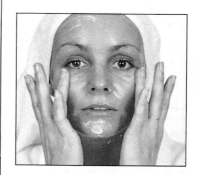

FACIAL MASSAGE 1 Always begin the massage with upward movements on neck to stimulate the blood supply

2 For maximum comfort, use either the palms of your hands or just fingertips to massage your forehead

3 To ease tension across the cheeks, place your fingertips on your nose and gently stroke your skin out to your ears

CLEANSING 1 Choose a light cream or liquid cleanser that suits your skin and spread it all over your face and neck

4 Any frown lines and wrinkles can be alleviated with gentle massaging in an upward rhythmical motion

5 Take particular care, when you massage the forehead, to cover the whole area right out to the hair line

6 When you have massaged around your mouth and eyes, give your eyebrows a gentle squeeze to release any tension

2 Rub the cleanser well into your face. Smooth it in well with fingertips always using upward movements

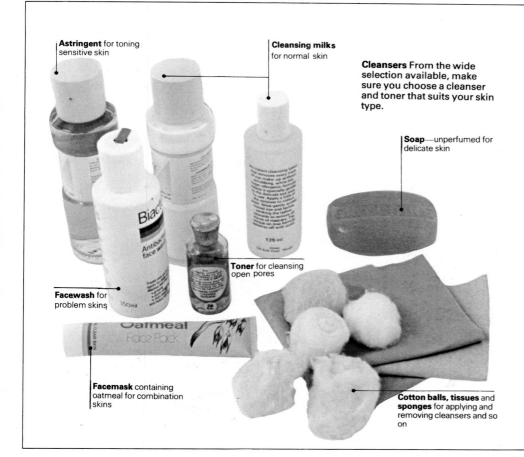

Astringent for toning sensitive skin

Cleansing milks for normal skin

Cleansers From the wide selection available, make sure you choose a cleanser and toner that suits your skin type.

Soap—unperfumed for delicate skin

Facewash for problem skins

Toner for cleansing open pores

Facemask containing oatmeal for combination skins

Cotton balls, tissues and **sponges** for applying and removing cleansers and so on

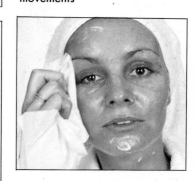

3 To remove the cleanser, gently wipe your face with a paper tissue taking care not to rub your skin harshly

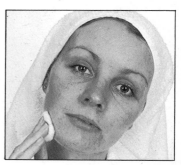

4 Either splash your face with cold water, or use a toner to stimulate your circulation and close up any open pores

face feeling vibrant and fresh. Never put a mask near your eyes where your skin is at its most delicate. There are many types of mask available over the counter — make sure you choose one that's right for your skin type.

If you want to make a mask at home, avocado mashed with a little olive oil provides ideal nourishment for a dry skin, while slivers of cucumber pressed lightly onto your face and over your eyelids are a good refresher. Ground oatmeal mixed to a paste with water will make an excellent scrub to get rid of dirt and dead skin.

A mask revitalises and refreshes the skin. Apply it evenly, avoiding the tender skin around the eyes, and plan to relax while you allow it to do its work. Removing the mask with cold water and cotton pads will make your skin tingle with life and health

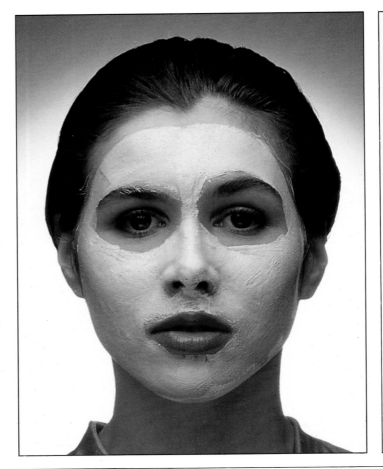

To measure your eyebrows, hold a pencil vertically along the line of your nose. If your brow line overlaps onto the bridge pluck the excess hair. If the line falls short, pencil it in. To find where the brow line should taper away, hold the pencil from the base of your nose across the corner of your eye.

The brow should finish in the same place as the tip of the pencil.

Eye care

When choosing an eye make-up remover, look for something that is alcohol-free, because it is less irritating to the eyes. Both lotions and pre-soaked cotton pads, which are ideal to put in your holiday travelling bag, are available in hypo-allergenic preparations. An inexpensive alternative is baby oil, but don't expect to be able to make-up again immediately after you have used it, as make-up won't go on over oil. Baby oil is best used at bed time.

Apply oils and lotions with a soft tissue — the filaments from cotton wool balls can get in the eyes and cause irritation. Wipe the remover gently over the browbone and lids. Allow 30 seconds for it to dissolve the shadow before wiping clean. Don't get impatient with your eyes and scrub at

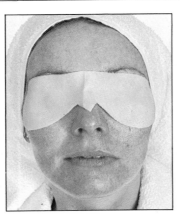

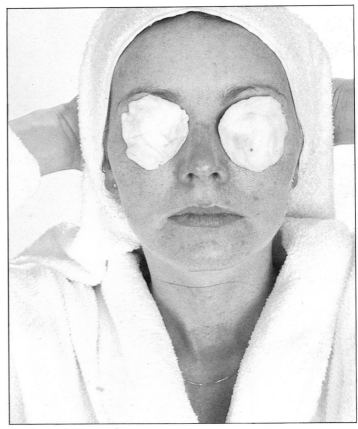

When you come to your beauty and cleansing routines, do not neglect your eyes, especially if you wear a lot of make-up on them. Always use a harmless make-up remover and use hypo-allergenic make-up if your eyes are sensitive. For tired or strained eyes, try relaxing with cool refreshing pads over them (above). Special eye-creams can also be beneficial. These are best applied thickly and then covered with dampened cotton balls (right)

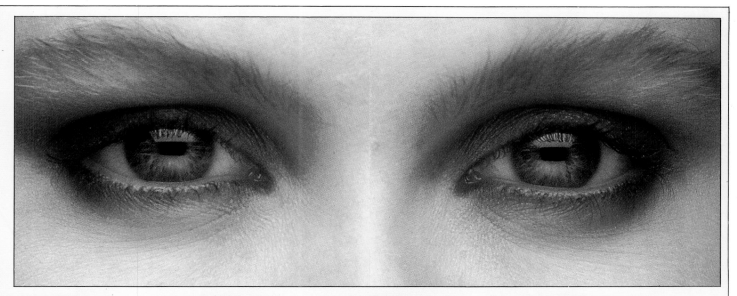

When plucking your eyebrows, carefully pluck both hair shaft and root

Brush your eyebrows upwards and outwards with firm strokes

Rid the eye area of oil or grime with a cotton cosmetic pad

Re-shaping eyebrows

Don't neglect the shape of your eyebrows. They can tell a great deal about your character and be highly expressive of your moods

them. Use a cotton bud to remove make-up from the corners of the eyes. Use a tissue soaked with remover to wipe the mascara from the eyelashes. When the eyes are clean, freshen up with a toner and splash with cold water to close the pores. Eyedrops will soothe the eyes and add sparkle. An eye cream massaged gently around the eyes at night will nourish the delicate skin in this area and help prevent the formation of wrinkles.

Take special care if you wear contact lenses. Avoid waterproof mascaras, mascaras with filaments and loose eyeshadow powders. These can all flake off into the eyes and cause irritation. Select a water-soluble mascara that has been tested hypo-allergenically for irritants and apply your eye make-up with a soft sponge applicator or cotton bud.

Skin Problems

Adolescence often causes problems for the complexion. Spots, blackheads and acne are all problems that beset a person whose hormonal balance is changing so that the glands produce too much sebum. These conditions do not mean that you have a dirty skin, but they can be minimised with careful and frequent washing with a mild soap to stop any bacteria spreading. A facial scrub will often remove blackheads, especially if you have opened the pores by steaming your face over a bowl of water first. You can help a spot to dry out more quickly by dabbing at it continually with antiseptic. This is a much better way of dealing with it than squeezing, which can result in bruising — an ugly red patch is hardly an improvement on a spot — bleeding and broken veins. If you have acne, you should see your doctor. Antibiotic treatment can often be prescribed, but, sadly, sometimes the only answer is: 'You'll grow out of it.' Check your diet and cut out sweet and greasy foods. Eat more fresh fruit and raw vegetables and drink plenty of mineral water. Keep your face scrupulously clean.

Unwanted hair can be dealt with in several ways: bleaching, shaving, waxing, depilation and epilation.

- Bleaching is very effective if you want to conceal a fine down of hair on face or arms. Do a patch test on your arm and leave it for an hour to make sure that there's no irritation before you apply the bleach to your face.
- Shaving removes hair quite satisfactorily from the underarms and the legs, but regrowth is quick and feels rough as the blunt end of the hair protrudes through the skin. You will need to shave regularly, with a shaving cream to avoid soreness. Don't apply deodorant to a shaved armpit straight away — it will sting.

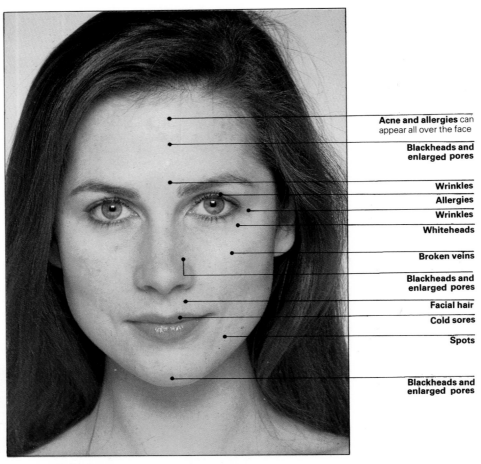

Acne and allergies can appear all over the face

Blackheads and enlarged pores

Wrinkles

Allergies

Wrinkles

Whiteheads

Broken veins

Blackheads and enlarged pores

Facial hair

Cold sores

Spots

Blackheads and enlarged pores

SKIN PROBLEMS The areas where problems are most likely to occur are indicated above. Blackheads may be prevented if you cleanse your face thoroughly. Wrinkles are less likely to form if your face is well moisturized. Broken veins are hard to remove, so hide them with make-up.

- Waxing can be done at home, but it's best to learn how by having the treatment done professionally first, as it's easy to burn yourself with the hot wax. Stripping off the wax is quite painful, but regrowth will not appear for about three weeks. Wax treatment is suitable for the legs and bikini line.
- Depilation is useful for underarm hair removal. A patch test with the depilatory cream is advisable to avoid soreness. These creams break off the hair shaft just below the skin. Wash thoroughly after use.
- Epilation is the only way of removing unwanted hair

Unwanted hair on the underarms and legs can be shaved — soften the skin with a shaving foam first — **or use a depilatory cream. Try out waxing in a salon before attempting it at home**

permanently, by electrolysis, and this must be done by an expert. Each hair is treated individually with a fine needle that has a electric current running through it. It's a lengthy and costly business but often worth it if you have, say, a heavy growth of coarse dark hair on your upper lip.

Understanding how spots develop

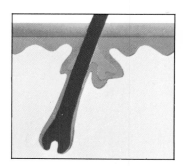

These diagrams show how a spot develops. In healthy skin, sebum is produced from the sebaceous gland near the hair follicle

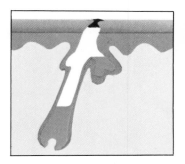

The excretion of sebum is hindered when the hair dies but the gland still continues to produce sebum

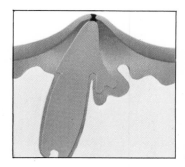

This results in the build-up of sebum that causes in turn a blackhead, a red spot or a whitehead

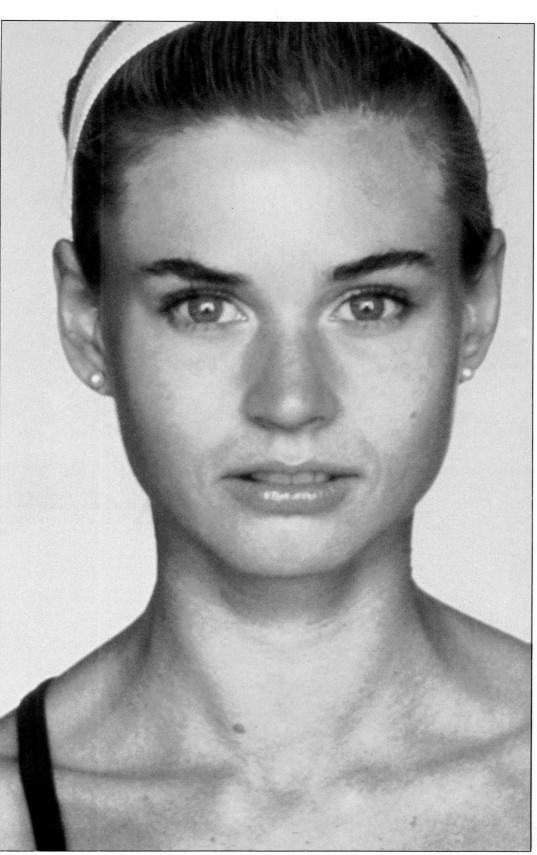

MAX FACTOR

Hand Care

Despite the harsh treatment they come in for, hands are one of the most neglected parts of the body. Very few women meet the requirements for a professional hand model: strong hands (hand modelling can be tiring) with long, slender fingers, tapered fingertips, narrow palms, and immaculately manicured nails. To keep their hands beautiful and preserve them from any damage, many hand models are careful to always wear gloves. Even if you don't have the long slender fingers of the professional hand model, you should keep your hands in flawless condition. Apply daily a hand cream or moisturizer, protect your hands from water and harsh weather by wearing gloves, keep nails well trimmed and have frequent manicures

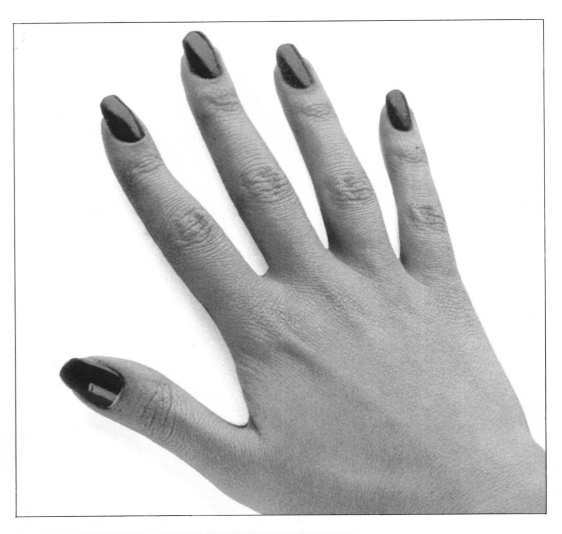

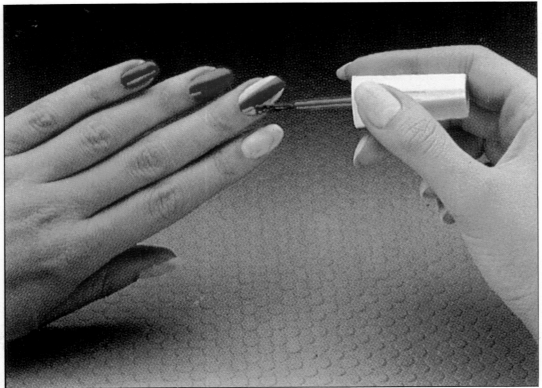

There are a few key steps to follow when applying nail polish. Always apply a base to your nails first. This will protect them from being stained by the polish. Let the base dry for five minutes. Roll the nail-polish bottle between your two palms. Do not shake it. Open the bottle and gently dip the brush in and out to gather enough polish for three nail strokes, applying the first stroke to the centre, the other two to the sides. Let the polish dry for 10 minutes and repeat with a second coat. After waiting 10 minutes, apply sealer to your nails and allow to dry for 20-30 minutes

A manicure once every two weeks is essential to keep your hands in tip-top condition. Women who work with their hands or whose hands are subjected to harsh chemicals or frequent wetting may need a manicure once a week. Assemble the following: cotton wool, nail polish remover, an emery board, petroleum jelly, baby oil, moisturizer, a soft tooth-brush and an orange stick

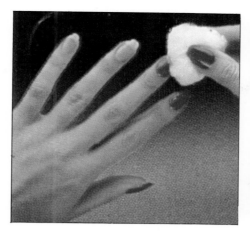

1 Remove all old polish with cotton cosmetic pads and nail-polish remover. Do not soak your nails before filing, as this will make them break more easily

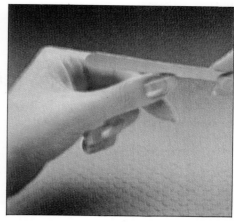

2 File each nail with an emery board by gently stroking from the side to the centre; do not file back and forth

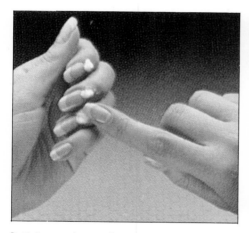

3 Rub petroleum jelly onto all of the cuticles and apply moisturizing cream to your nails and hands

4 Now, warm three-quarters of a cup of baby oil on the stove. Do not boil. Pour into a small bowl and soak your fingertips in the oil for five minutes

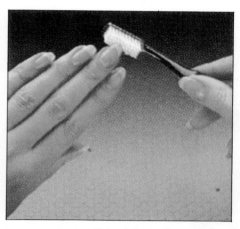

5 With a soft toothbrush, remove any matter from underneath your nails. Rinse your hands under warm water and dry off thoroughly

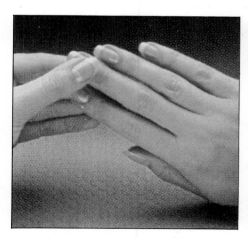

6 Using your fingertips, train your cuticles back

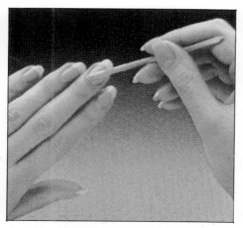

7 With the blunt end of an orange stick, train the cuticles back again. Never try to cut your cuticles

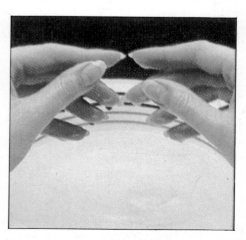

8 Rinse your hands again in warm water and remove any traces of baby oil. Your manicure is now complete. If you are going to apply polish to your nails, you should wait for five minutes

Foot Care

To forestall foot troubles and keep your feet looking attractive, give yourself a pedicure once every two weeks. If you happen to walk or exercise a great deal, you may need one every week. Just as before a manicure, remove all traces of polish from your toes

1 Wash each foot in turn in soapy water, but do not soak feet

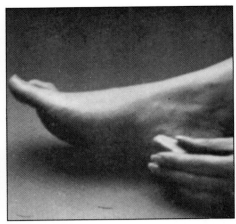

2 With a pumice stone, gently rub the soles and heels to shed hard skin

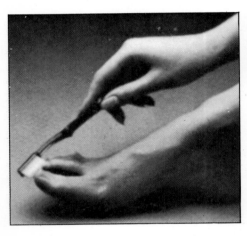

3 Use a soft toothbrush to remove debris from underneath and around the nails

4 Dry your feet thoroughly, especially between your toes

5 Always trim the nails with a toenail clipper or nail scissors, cutting straight across

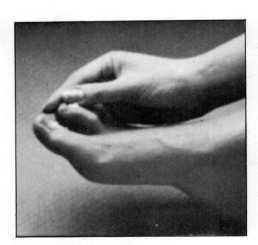

6 Apply petroleum jelly to the base and sides of the nails with your fingertips

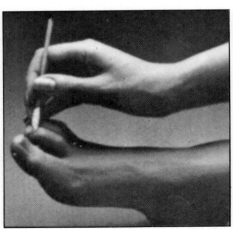

7 With the blunt end of an orange stick, work at the base and sides of your nails to ease the skin back

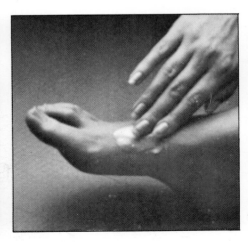

8 Finally rub some moisturizer onto the top and bottom of your feet and onto your toes

Foot problems are usually self-inflicted. The best way to prevent them is to wear comfortable, well-fitting shoes, not the platform soles, stiletto heels or pointed shoes that may happen to be in fashion. Keep these points in mind when buying shoes:

1. Any shoe you buy should be 1cm (½in) longer than your foot and should provide plenty of room for you to wriggle your toes.

2. Shoes must fit perfectly round the heels

3. Shoes should not pinch, rub and squeeze any part of the foot and should provide plenty of support for your arch. Never buy a tight-fitting shoe and expect it to 'give'

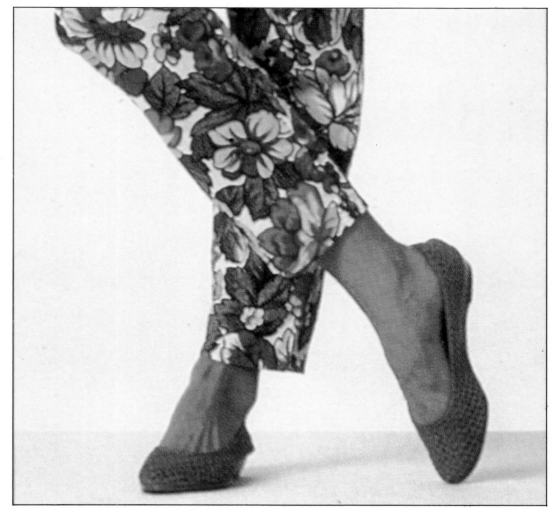

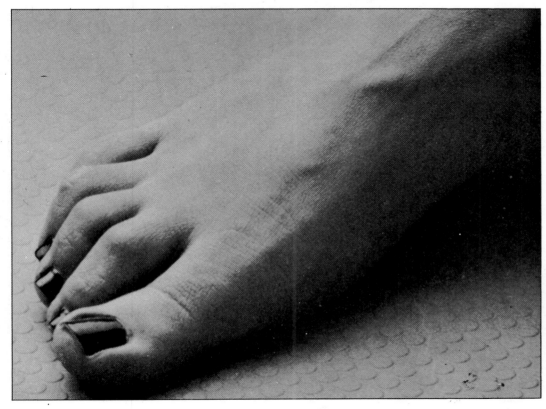

To round off your pedicure, apply a touch of nail varnish. Avoid chipped, peeling nail varnish by applying one layer of base coat to clean nails, followed by two layers of colour. Allow each layer to dry thoroughly

Chapter 4

Making up

Always begin your make-up routine by cleansing, toning and moisturising the skin. Make-up applied to skin that is not scrupulously clean will clog the pores, besides looking stale and unattractive. Whether you cleanse with a cream, a foam or a mild soap and warm water, a toner will put life and freshness into your skin and close the pores. Splashing your face with cold water will produce a similar effect. If you have a dry or sensitive skin choose a toner that does not contain alcohol. More astringent preparations can be used on oily skins. If your forehead and nose tend to be greasy and the rest of your face is dry, you would be wise to use two different preparations.

Moisturisers are important to nourish and protect the skin. They leave it soft and smooth so that foundation can be applied evenly. To warm up a sallow skin, use a moisturiser that is slightly mauve-tinted. A greenish one will calm down a florid complexion, and a rosy one bring to life a pallid face. Use tinted conditioners very sparingly so as not to end up with a green or mauve face.

MAX FACTOR

Use your make-up with skill to reflect your mood and your lifestyle. Soft and natural make-up for day wear can be replaced with something daringly dramatic for evening

Inside your make-up box

Anyone who wants to be proficient in the art of make-up today will find a vast and exciting range of cosmetics to choose from. Be prepared to make a few mistakes before you find out which particular beauty products suit you. Remember that your requirements may change with age, but basically you will need, apart from your skin-care kit of cleansers, toners and moisturizers, to equip yourself.

● A box of tissues and a packet of cotton buds for blotting and correcting mistakes. Cotton wool is not as useful near the eyes — fibres of it can get caught in the lashes and dragged into the eye.

● To apply make-up you will need sponges and brushes. Packets of small sea sponges are ideal for spreading foundation. They are long lasting and do not stain. For powder you can choose a soft, broad brush or an old-fashioned puff made of velvet or down, any of which will apply the powder finely. For the eyes you will need a shadow brush of medium thickness or a sponge applicator. A short, fat blusher brush and a chisel-shaped lip brush complete this section of your make-up bag. When buying brushes remember that quality matters. Make sure the bristles are of even length and do not pull away with a gentle tug. Keep brushes and sponges clean by washing in a mild soap solution, rinsing well and leaving to dry where fresh air can easily circulate around them.

● Foundation. You can choose from liquid, cream or solid foundation, which comes in a stick. Liquid foundations are light but they tend to streak, and creams are generally best for a normal skin. Sticks are useful for covering spots and blemishes. Choose a warm pink tone for a sallow skin. To tone down a too-pink skin, choose a beige colour. A highly coloured complexion can be toned down with a greenish base to a beige foundation. Olive skins and dark skins rarely need corrective colouring — just plenty of moisturizer to counteract dryness.

● Powder. Although this is available in many shades and textures, the lightest and most translucent is best for a natural fresh look. Powder will keep foundation from streaking and is especially useful if your nose and forehead tend to shine. Avoid a caked look by applying powder very lightly and brushing off the excess with a fine soft brush.

● Blusher. One of the most important items in your beauty box. Skilfully used, it can transform the shape of your face, minimizing the prominence of features you'd like to disguise and drawing attention to your best points. Choose a cream blusher for use on a cream foundation, and powder for a heavier foundation. Two colours, one slightly darker than the other, can be blended into each other on the cheekbones for a more dramatic effect.

● Eyeshadow. There is a huge variety of colours to choose from and with a minimum outlay you can equip yourself with everything from subtle shades of grey and fawn, through delicate blues and greens to stronger harvest colours and striking pinks and purples. Add gold, silver and glitter for extra glamour. Choose your eyeshadow to suit your eye colour, to reflect your mood and to complement your

clothes. If you find that cream eyeshadow tends to streak, try applying a very fine dusting of translucent powder on top of it.

• Eyeliner. A good kohl stick will produce both a clear line and a more subtle smudged effect. You will need a pencil sharpener, but always make sure that you round off the end of the kohl to avoid hurting the delicate skin around the eye. A liquid liner will give a more clearly defined effect. You can experiment with various colours, but black is the most useful basic.

• Mascara. Most women prefer the liquid mascara that you apply with a wand as it is less messy than the solid cake variety. If you choose the type with added fibres to thicken the lashes, you may need an eyelash comb to remove bits that stick in the wrong places. A mascara without added fibres is normally sufficient to make lashes look long and lustrous when applied correctly. For a dramatic effect, or for fun, you may like to try false eyelashes. Fixing them in position needs practice — unless you get them exactly right they'll look awful — and they do have a tendency to curl up at the ends and drop off at the wrong moments. Try an eyelash curler used in conjunction with lots of mascara instead.

• For the eyebrows, the most essential thing is a good pair of tweezers to remove stray hairs and give the brows the shape you want. A soft brown pencil will darken the hairs, but be careful not to colour your skin unless you want to create an unnatural effect.

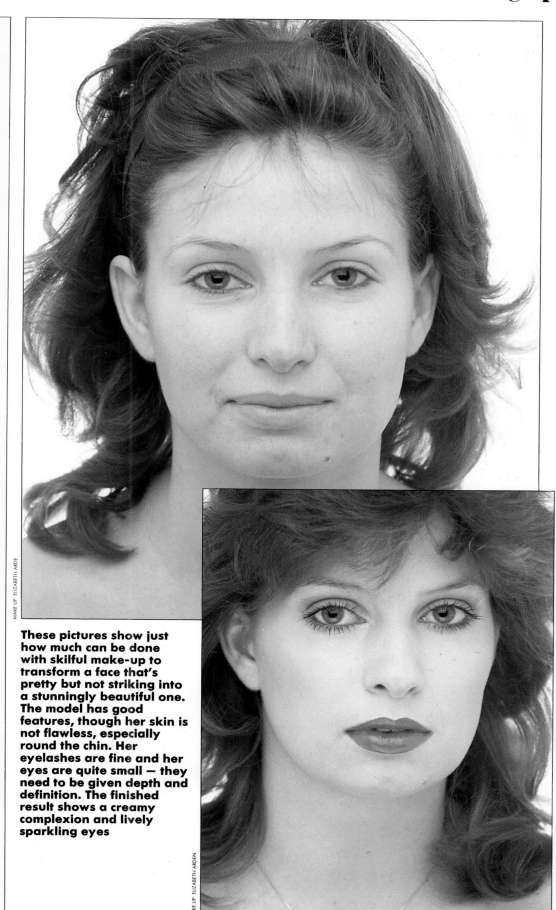

MAKE UP: ELIZABETH ARDEN

These pictures show just how much can be done with skilful make-up to transform a face that's pretty but not striking into a stunningly beautiful one. The model has good features, though her skin is not flawless, especially round the chin. Her eyelashes are fine and her eyes are quite small — they need to be given depth and definition. The finished result shows a creamy complexion and lively sparkling eyes

MAKE UP: ELIZABETH ARDEN

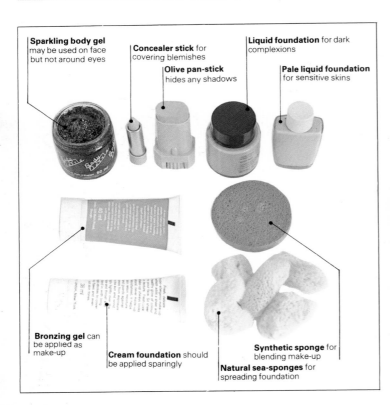

Sparkling body gel may be used on face but not around eyes

Concealer stick for covering blemishes

Olive pan-stick hides any shadows

Liquid foundation for dark complexions

Pale liquid foundation for sensitive skins

Bronzing gel can be applied as make-up

Cream foundation should be applied sparingly

Synthetic sponge for blending make-up

Natural sea-sponges for spreading foundation

CONCEALER A concealing cream a little lighter than the foundation is applied **under the model's eyes to hide dark circles and a slight bagging effect**

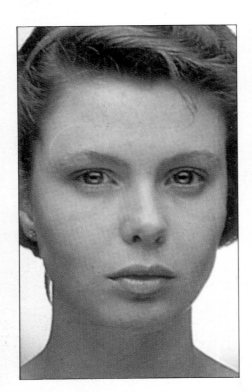

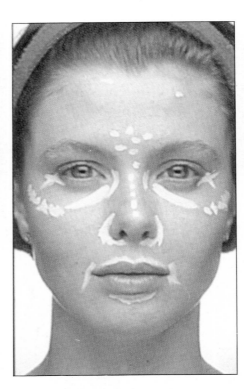

FOUNDATION 1 About five minutes before applying foundation, put a thin coating of moisturiser on your face to help spread the colour evenly. Use a tiny, slightly damp sponge or your fingertips to apply foundation

2 Dot circles on eyelids, under eyes, on forehead, the centre of your nose, cheeks and under your chin. Blend the liquid into the skin with a quick, light touch. Do not rub it in as this can clog the pores

3 Blend the foundation onto your neck with long strokes that stop at the collar bone. Finally, take a tissue and cover your face lightly; the tissue will absorb any excess foundation. Lean your head forward and shake the tissue off

Foundation

If you are lucky enough to have a perfect complexion you will not need a foundation, but even the most beautiful skins can misbehave and a foundation will even out skin tones. Foundations are available in liquids or gels, creams or solid sticks and cakes. Your foundation should be as light as possible — indeed it should not be obvious that you are wearing one. Mask-like faces are very ageing — your skin looks its best when it feels alive and glowing with health. The colour of your foundation is important — it should blend as closely as possible with your skin tone to avoid a jarring change of colour at the jawline. Take your time in choosing before you buy, and use the testers on display at the make-up counter. Ideally, these should be tried out on your face, and not on the back of your hand, which is almost certainly going to be very different in colour. Look at the results in daylight rather than in the artificial light of the shop.

To apply the foundation, dot it sparingly over the centre of the face and spread it evenly over the skin with a small sponge moistened with water. Use gentle upward and outward strokes. Finish off round the hair- and jawline with your fingertips to make sure there is no visible edge and no foundation clinging to the hair. If your skin is blemished you can use a cover stick to hide the offending spot. Pat it on and blend the edges in to tone with the rest of your skin.

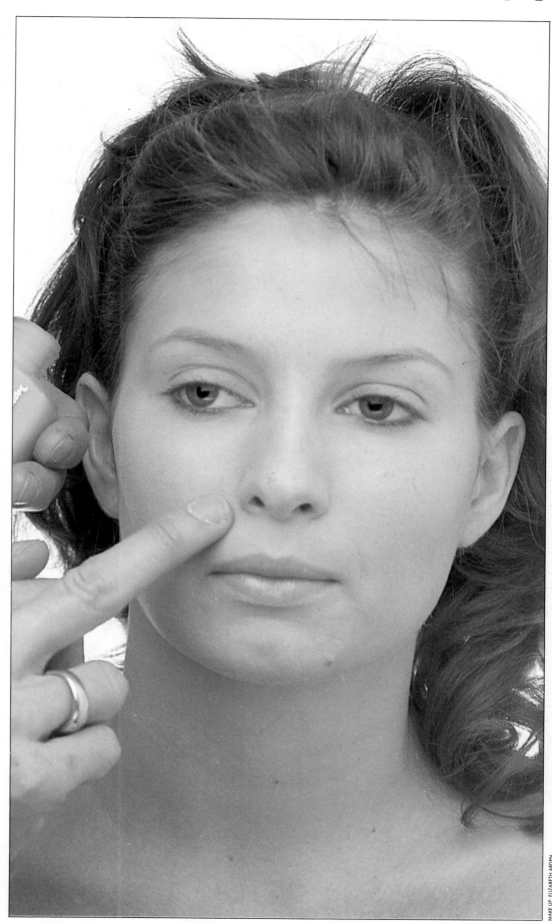

Concealer is applied under the foundation to correct irregularities in the model's complexion around the nose and chin — problem areas for many women

Blusher and powder

Once you have experimented with blusher you will realise that it plays an essential part in the art of make-up. It flatters with colour and with shape too, and careful use of blusher can make the most of your looks. Blusher in the form of a gel should be applied on top of your moisturiser — don't add powder or you will spoil the gel's translucent shine. Cream blusher is applied over moisturiser or foundation and followed by powder. Powder blusher should be applied over face powder. Gels and creams can be dotted onto the face and blended in with the fingertips, powders dusted on gently with a fat brush. To find out what colour blusher will suit you best, pinch your cheeks and copy the shade of your natural blush. For a highlighter, choose pale peach or ivory for fair skins. If you are dark-skinned or have a tan, gold looks stunning, especially for evening wear.

The positioning of blusher and highlighter is vital. For a heart-shaped face, highlight the cheekbones. The blusher goes on under the cheekbones, sweeping up towards the top of the ear. Broaden a pointed chin with blusher at the tip and highlighter just above it on either side. An oval face needs only gentle shading to emphasise the cheekbones. A round face that tends to plumpness can be made to look thinner by shading the jawline, the cheeks and above the browbone. To reduce the width of the nose, highlight the tip and the sides of it. A square face can be softened by shading from the jawline to the cheeks, and again on the temples.

Blusher is applied to the model's cheeks in a diagonal line from the corner of her eye to the tip of her ear

Brown pressed powder for shading

White powder for highlights

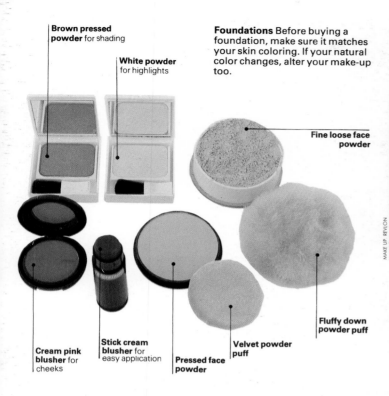

Foundations Before buying a foundation, make sure it matches your skin coloring. If your natural color changes, alter your make-up too.

Fine loose face powder

Cream pink blusher for cheeks

Stick cream blusher for easy application

Pressed face powder

Velvet powder puff

Fluffy down powder puff

MAKE UP REVLON

Blusher can completely transform the shape of your face. Here the model slims her cheeks, at the same time emphasising her cheek bone and giving a healthy glow to her face

The model is applying blusher to her jawline to create more definition

The best way to apply powder is with a soft fat brush. A fine dusting of translucent powder gives the face a smooth satiny finish and evens out any irregularities in the complexion that may not be disguised by the foundation

MAKE UP ELIZABETH ARDEN

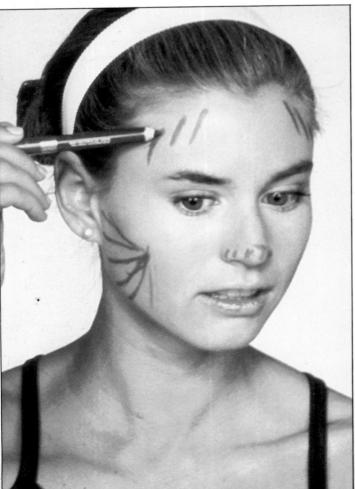

Highlighting is as important as shading to give definition to good bone structure. Here a pearly highlighter is used on the cheekbones to complement the rose pinks, violets and cyclamen of the model's other make-up colours

To narrow a broad forehead, slim the cheek and create definition on the cheekbone, the model draws stripes on her face with a shader crayon. The marks on the tip of the nose will reduce its length. Blended in, these lines will subtly alter the shape of her face

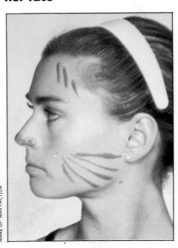

Changing the shape of your face

● Forehead. A high and broad forehead is best disguised by changing your hairstyle, but make-up can also help. Choose a rosy blusher and shade at the temples and down the hairline towards the eyes. Go gently to avoid making a hard line and check your handiwork to make sure that particles of blusher are not clogging the hair. Blend well.

● Nose. To narrow the bridge of the nose, draw a fine line with shader down the side of your nose from your eyebrow, stopping when you reach the level of the outer corner of the eye. Blend the shadow carefully. To make the nose look more slender, continue the line from the bridge to the bottom of the nose just above the nostril. Blend carefully. If your nose looks too flat, brush a light brown blusher down either side and around the nostrils. Blend a thin line of highlighter down the centre of your nose. To make large nostrils look smaller, apply shader in a thin line with an eyeliner brush in a crescent moon shape around the crease at the side of each nostril. The contour should be widest and darkest at the nostrils. Be sure to blend the line in well so that it is invisible.

MAKE UP: REVLON

MAKE UP: MAX FACTOR

MAKE UP: MAX FACTOR

● Chin. To highlight a firm chin or define a receding one, brush cream-toned highlighter on the point of the chin and blend it in. To soften a pointed chin, apply highlighter under the corners of the mouth in the hollows at each side of your chin. Do not blend yet. Now apply a dot of shader on the point of the chin and blend in all three spots of colour, starting with the shader.

● Cheeks. To narrow a broad face, apply shader on the fullest part of your cheeks, between the cheek and jawbone. Start the shader just below the centre of the eye and angle it upwards, towards the centre of your ear. Blend well. Now brush on highlighter in a diagonal line above the cheekbones from the outer corner of the eye to the hairline. Widen the diagonal area as you work out towards the hairline and the top of the ear. Blend in well.

Eyes

Your eyes are your first and most important contact with another person. They are most expressive of your character and emotions and even if you choose to wear little other make-up normally, you probably like to emphasise your eyes. You need to exercise care and be delicate in your application of make-up here — even a dramatic effect is best achieved subtly and with allure. Start with the eyeshadow, remembering to keep all your brushes and applicators clean to avoid irritation or infection.

The most popular kind of eyeshadow is pressed powder, but there are also loose powders, creams, gels, sticks and pencils. Pressed powders are easy to apply with a brush or sponge-tipped applicator.

The model's eyelids are subtly coloured, shading into a darker crease in the socket of the eye. Now a pearly highlighter is applied under the brow to give increased definition

MAKE UP ELIZABETH ARDEN

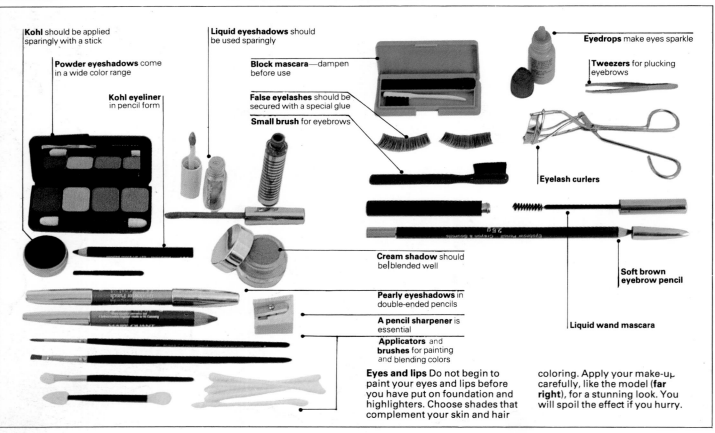

Kohl should be applied sparingly with a stick

Powder eyeshadows come in a wide color range

Kohl eyeliner in pencil form

Liquid eyeshadows should be used sparingly

Block mascara—dampen before use

False eyelashes should be secured with a special glue

Small brush for eyebrows

Eyedrops make eyes sparkle

Tweezers for plucking eyebrows

Eyelash curlers

Cream shadow should be blended well

Pearly eyeshadows in double-ended pencils

A pencil sharpener is essential

Applicators and **brushes** for painting and blending colors

Soft brown eyebrow pencil

Liquid wand mascara

Eyes and lips Do not begin to paint your eyes and lips before you have put on foundation and highlighters. Choose shades that complement your skin and hair

coloring. Apply your make-up carefully, like the model (**far right**), for a stunning look. You will spoil the effect if you hurry.

Loose powders come in vibrant colours — but you will need to moisten the sponge-tipped applicator to get these to hold. Creams and gels are best blended into the shape you want with the tip of the finger. If you are using a pencil colour on the eye, first draw in the shape you want, then blend it with your fingertip. Add highlighter under the eyebrow and on the cheekbone below the outer corner of the eye.

The next step is eyeliner. Carefully paint a fine line close to the lashes, above the upper ones and beneath the lower ones, and colour the rims of the eyes with kohl. Then comes mascara. Whichever type you choose, it always pays to take your time. Several lightly applied coats, with time in between for each to dry, look much more effective than one thick one. Stroke the mascara wand carefully upwards through the upper lashes and downwards through the lower ones. Zigzag the wand gently to avoid clogging. Smudges can be removed with a moist cotton bud; blobs on the lashes with an eyelash brush or comb.

Now brush your eyebrows, first upwards and then into their natural shape. Stray hairs below the brow should be removed when you take your make-up off, but if you spot the odd one, hold the skin taut around it and tweeze it out smartly but gently in the direction of the hair growth. Soft strokes of the eyebrow pencil define the brow. Brush again to disguise the pencil work.

Mascara is applied for longer-looking, darker and more luxuriant lashes. A wand applicator is easiest to use. Apply several coats, waiting in between for each one to dry

Combining eyeshadow colours

- For dark eyes, try mauve, rose and silver grey; canary yellow, beige and gold; or ivory, navy blue and turquoise.
- For hazel eyes, try pale brown, copper highlighter and rust brown; pale pink, lilac and deep purple; or almond brown, silver grey and khaki.
- For green eyes, try gold highlighter, pale orange and red gold; bone, bronze and khaki; or pale grey, electric blue and yellow gold.
- For brown eyes, try grey blue, lilac and grape purple; salmon pink, pink gold and deep rose; or pale gold, brick red and medium brown.
- For blue grey eyes, try pink lilac, mauve highlighter, and plum; white, greyish purple and dark grey; or white, jade green and smoky blue.

Apply eye-drops to soothe sore or bloodshot eyes

Define the eye area with a thin dusting of translucent powder

Draw a pencil line on the inside of the lower lid above the lash line

Apply a pale shade over the top lid with a sponge applicator

Highlight the brow line with a soft ivory shade

Apply mascara using zigzag movements for lower lashes

Carefully pencil in your eyebrow shape with light strokes

Brush eyebrows upwards into a gentle arch with a small brush

Changing the shape of your eyes

Before applying any eye make-up, use a concealing cream if necessary around the eyes to hide blemishes that won't be disguised by eyeshadow. Blend this in with the fingertips. Then dust with a thin film of translucent powder, brushing excess away with a small soft brush. Line the lower rims of the eyes with kohl to emphasise the brilliance of the whites. Now you are ready to apply your chosen eyeshadow — use two shades for well-defined eyes with good shape and depth. Skilful use of eyeshadow can correct the shape of your eyes.

1 Small eyes. To enlarge small eyes, brush on a light coloured powdered shadow with an angle-tipped brush just above your lashes. Apply a darker shadow near the crease. Don't colour near the inner corner of your eye — this will make your eyes look smaller. When applying shadow at the sides, use your brush to blend the powdered shades into one another. Use a light grey pencil under the eye to create a wide-eyed look.

2 Wide-set eyes. With a small blusher brush, apply contour powder that is slightly darker than your skin tone between the eyes and the bridge of your nose. Brush and blend the powder down the sides of your nose. Next brush a neutral-toned highlighter under the outside edge of the brow. Shade the crease line, emphasising the inside corner of the eye near the nose. Finish by brushing a light matt shadow on the outer corner of the eye.

3 Almond eyes. Brush a light-coloured shadow onto your brow bone. Blend in a

colour that is a few shades darker on your eyelid. Line the lower inside rim of the eye with black or brown kohl pencil, extending the line out to the corner of your eye. If you have blue eyes, use a blue pencil.

4 Close-set eyes. Brush a pale highlighter on the inside corner of the eyes and blend carefully into the side of the nose to make your eyes seem further apart. Next brush a dark-toned shadow onto the outside third of your brow bone, shaping upwards and outwards. If you want maximum definition line the lower rims of the eyes with black kohl pencil.

5 Protruding eyes. Shade the entire lid with a medium- to deep-coloured eyeshadow. Never use frosted shades or highlighters, as they will emphasise your prominent brow bones and protruding eye sockets. Apply kohl pencil on the lower rims of the eyes. Curl your eyelashes or wear mascara on only the centre lashes.

6 Deep-set eyes. To make deep-set eyes more prominent, brush a pale pink or beige shadow over the eyelid and fade it out above the hollow of the crease. Then apply a medium-toned eyeshadow, starting at the brow bone and blending it up into the brow. Darken the eye area directly over the natural crease with a smoky-coloured shadow that blends well with your other choices. Line the inside lower rims of the eyes with black or brown kohl pencil.

7 Drooping eyes. Starting at the inside corner of the eye, brush a medium-toned shadow upwards and outwards, stopping just short of the brow line. Don't brush any colour on the outer edge of the lid

1

1

2

3

4

5

6

7

8

9

where the eye begins to droop. Instead, create a crease line that is slightly higher than your own by shading it with taupe or medium brown eyeshadow. Curling the lashes will make your eyes look less droopy, as will a few carefully applied coats of mascara.

8 Round eyes. Choose a deep-coloured shadow and apply it starting at the inside corner of the eye. Blend the colour in an upward angle towards the outer edge of the brow. Intensify the colour in the corner of the eye and lessen it as you work up towards the brow. Apply a lighter toned shadow or pencil under the lower lid, and extend the colour up and out to blend with the colour below. Dust pale highlighter near the brow line.

9 Oriental eyes. Brush a pale matt eyeshadow over the entire lid. Pale pink works well and is a colour traditionally favoured by Oriental women. Now apply a medium toned eyeshadow on the inner corner of the eye, intensifying the colour closest to the bridge of the nose. Continue blending towards the centre of your eye until the shadow fades out, then brush a darker shade on the outer corner of the eye. Keep the colour most intense near the lid. Blend from the outer corner of the lid in an arc towards the outer edge of the eyebrow. Also blend subtly towards the nose to merge the colours. Apply kohl eyeliner to the lower rims of the eyes. The finer the line, the more depth it will give to your eyes. A slash of colour will only emphasise the slant of your eyes and make them seem heavier. Finally, smudge the area below the outside of the lower lashes with kohl in a subtle tone.

Lips

Your lips at their best are expressive and sensual. Lipstick should enhance these qualities, making them moist, supple, glossy and rosy — never cracked and dry. You can easily improve the shape of your lips by drawing a new outline with a lip pencil or brush. Your choice of lip colour can determine the balance of your face. A lighter, more natural shade of lipstick will allow the attention to be focussed on the eyes, but if you want to try a different effect, go for a richer, darker lipstick and minimal eye make-up. The best method of applying lipstick is with a lip brush. You will need a steady hand and a little practice, but a brush does give the cleanest and most accurate line, and it is also very economical.

The lipstick always goes on after the powder, and the fine coat of powder around the mouth helps prevent the lip colour bleeding upwards in tiny lines. Draw on the outline with a pencil or lip brush, using a slightly darker colour than the one you have chosen to fill in with. Now fill in the lips — again a brush is best for this. Blot carefully with a tissue and apply a second coat of lipstick or a generous coat of gloss, being careful not to take it too close to the outline as it may make the lipstick run.

Nails

Always keep your nails scrupulously clean and smoothly shaped. The cuticles should be pushed back neatly. Remember that your hands are often seen close to your face — badly manicured or neglected nails will ruin the effect of the most sophisticated make-up. If you paint your nails, you need not choose exactly the same shade as your lips as long as the two colours complement each other. If you don't like nail varnish, you can buy a special nail cream from the chemist and buff it up with a chamois buffer for a natural healthy shine. A white pencil can be effective applied under the tips of the nails.

MAKE-UP: ELIZABETH ARDEN

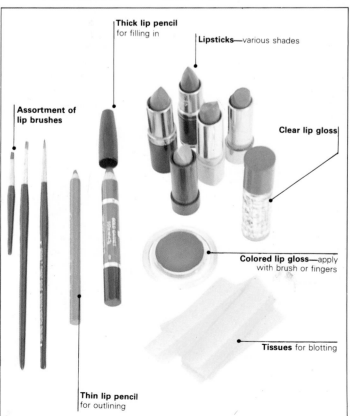

Thick lip pencil
for filling in

Lipsticks—various shades

Assortment of
lip brushes

Clear lip gloss

Colored lip gloss—apply
with brush or fingers

Tissues for blotting

Thin lip pencil
for outlining

Lipstick always looks more professional when applied with a lip brush. The outline of the lips is drawn first, and then filled in. It's a more economical way of using lipstick, too

Enhancing your normal lip definition

If lipstick is applied alone, without a lip pencil outline, the resulting splash of colour can make your lips look more imbalanced than they are. Use lip pencils for framing your lips to their best advantage. Remember that your lips should be dry when you apply lipstick

1 Moisturise

2 To define normal lips, use your pencil to draw the outline in small, quick strokes, starting at the brow on the upper lip. This outline also helps to prevent lipstick from smearing

3 Continue the outline towards each corner of your mouth, keeping it closed and free of tension. Fill in the outline of the bottom lip and prepare the lip brush with colour

4 Brush in colour, starting at the centre of your lip and working outwards; repeat on your lower lip. Depending on the effect you want to achieve, smudge the pencil outline to blend with the lip colour, or leave the outline half visible

5 For extra shine, dab silver highlighter on the middle of your lower lip. Always blot lips with a tissue

Changing the shape of your lips

• **Thin lips.** If you keep lipstick to the natural outline of thin lips, your lips can look mean and hard. You will need to draw a new outline to make them look fuller. First select a lip colour and a lip pencil that is a shade darker for outlining. Define the bow of your upper lip with the pencil in two precise even strokes. Carry the lines of the bow down to the corners of your mouth. Keep your mouth closed and relaxed. Rest your elbow on the dressing table for a steady hand. Use precise short strokes of the pencil rather than attempting to draw a single continuous line. Repeat with the lower lip, starting at the centre and working out towards the corners. To avoid a hard outline, gently smudge the line you have drawn towards the inside of your lips. Now take some colour onto your lip brush and colour in the outline with soft short strokes. Start at the centre of your mouth and work towards the corners, then open your mouth and brush the lip colour inwards to avoid a hard line. If one lip is lighter than the other, apply a dab of foundation to it before you put on your lipstick.

• **Full lips.** Outline just within the edge of your lips with a lip pencil to minimise full lips. Start at the centre of the upper lip and stroke down towards each corner. Now do the same for the lower lip. Put some colour that is a shade lighter than the pencil onto the lip brush and fill in your lips, starting at the centre and working out towards the corners. The best colours to use to minimise full lips are light rosy shades.

• **Thin upper lip; full lower lip.** To give your lips an even fullness, draw an outline beyond the outer edge of your upper lip with the lip pencil, starting at the bow and proceeding with small light strokes to the corners. Follow the natural outline of your lower lip. Fill in the lips with colour on a lip brush.

• **Wide lips.** If wide lips bother you, then outline them with a dark-toned lip pencil, fading the line towards the corners of your nouth. Fill in with slightly lighter lip colour. Smudge the outline so that it blends with the lipstick. Avoid shiny or bright lipstick and never wear lip gloss, as these will give the illusion of larger lips.

The finishing touches have been applied to the model's make-up — her eyes look soft and dewy, her lashes thick and lustrous, and the make-up artist has made the most of her full lips

MAKE UP ELIZABETH ARDEN

Make-up and Skin Colour

Pale skin

Always use a delicate hand when making up a pale skin and choose the lightest possible colours. Draw attention to the eyes with a kohl pencil and mascara, but avoid a heavy eyeshadow — the faintest shades of grey and smoky blue will suit you best. An almost translucent peaches-and-cream foundation followed by a light dusting of the finest powder will enhance an English rose complexion. Use a rosy blusher to emphasise your cheekbones and a pale colourless lip gloss. A touch of silver or gold will suit you for evening wear.

Your skin is very vulnerable and you should protect it carefully from harsh weather conditions. Don't expose your skin to the sun if you can possibly help it — you are almost bound to burn. Protect yourself with a sun screen: PF (protein factor) 6-10. If you want a healthy glowing look, use a bronze gel to give a gently tanned effect.

Fair skin

Moisturiser is very important for you, as your skin probably tends towards dryness. You will burn rather than tan, so keep yourself well protected from the sun. Use a sun screen with PF 5 and expect freckles to appear, especially along the nose and across the cheeks. Choose a light foundation and smoky colours for the eyes — as long as you aren't heavy-handed with your make-up, almost any colour should suit you.

This is a very stunning look for evening, but it has been achieved with natural shades that complement the model's warm skin and hair tones. Blusher has been used to slim her face and emphasise her cheekbones

The model's dark skin is complemented by a tawny blusher, russet eyeshadow and brick red lipstick. Her eyes are emphasised with kohl and lashes thickly fringed with mascara (left)

A medium skin can take a rich red lipstick and dark eyes are not overwhelmed by strong colours, such as the deep indigo and plum used here. A warm blusher completes this glowing look (right)

Medium to olive skin

You have the perfect background upon which to create a dramatic effect — scarlet lips and dull greenish-gold eyeshadow with lashings of mascara will not overwhelm your classic complexion. If you prefer more subtle colours, go for warmer shades — coral or tawny lips with bronze or harvest highlighter and smudged kohl around the eyes. A mauve-tinted moisturiser will counteract a tendency to sallowness and a creamy highlighter under the brows will enhance the depth of your eyes. Avoid sugary lip colours and pastels for the eyes — these are best left to fairer skins.

MAKE-UP: MAX FACTOR, COLORFAST "SPICE OF LIFE"

Dark skins

A bronze gel is often all you need to give your complexion a healthy glow, but if your skin is patchy, stick to brown tones and avoid pinks. Highlight your cheekbones with brick- or orange-toned blusher. Go for warmth and richness too when choosing eye colour: amber, gold, copper, amethyst, plum and wine will all suit you. If your lips are not too full you can go to town with brilliant fruity pinks (avoid lilac tones) or rich reds, but fuller lips look better with subtler, more natural lip colour — or none at all, so that all the emphasis is placed on the eyes.

Black skins

Black skins tend to be greasy, but when exposed to cold weather they can also suffer from dryness. If your complexion is good, a moisturiser or bronze gel is all you'll need to make your skin glow with health. A patchy skin will need a light foundation — your choice here is important, as the luminescent quality of black skin is one of its best attributes; the last thing you want to do is clog the pores and end up looking as if you're wearing a mask. There are special products for black skin, and the darker shades of most cosmetic ranges will suit you too.

Experiment with highlighter in palest pink blended well into your foundation — a pearlised one will enhance the polish of your skin. Pearlised colours are perfect for your eyes as well — try gold, amethyst, deep burgundy and blushing rose. Emphasise the brilliance of the whites of your eyes with a bold line of kohl on the rims and use several coats of mascara, waiting until each coat dries before applying the next. For evening, glitter looks wonderful on black skin. You can use the most vivid greens and blues on your eyes and your lips can be as bright and luscious as you like — you'll be able to get away with extravagant shades that would overwhelm a paler skin.

Redheads

Red hair and freckles often go together. This is because redheads have less melanin, the brown pigment in the skin, and so the skin is translucent and flecked with brown. Your skin will burn easily, so protect it with a sun screen with PF 5. A sun screen will minimise the appearance of freckles (they fade in the winter anyway), but most people find freckles attractive because they make the skin look so healthy. A bronze gel will give your skin a deep lustrous glow. You may like to use a light cover-up foundation for a more sophisticated evening look. Your natural colours are warm tawny ones. Avoid blue, silver and sugary pinks, but olive greens and khakis will suit your eyes and, if you want a change, try scarlet or strong raspberry on your lips.

Oriental skin

If your skin is pale, it will be creamy; darker skins veer towards olive tones. You will need only a light foundation, and it can be either pinkish or tawny. You can afford to emphasise your almond eye shape with a fine black liner and go for really exotic colours for lips and eyes, such as cyclamen pink, bright blue and gold; or you can choose a more subtle and mysterious look with smudged kohl around the eyes, smoky mauve and sea green shadow, amber blusher and warm ginger lips with extra gloss. Orientals often have small eyes, and heavy mascara will only make them appear smaller. Concentrate on the shape of your eyes rather than on your lashes.

47

Chapter 5

Your Hair

A flattering hairstyle can be the most important single factor in your appearance. Not only does it tell about your character, it balances your body, frames your face and complements your clothes and lifestyle. A really professional haircut is a valuable investment, because it will make you feel good as well as look good.

When choosing a new hairstyle you should look carefully at the shape of your face. Try this when shampooing your hair. Lather it up onto the top of your head, put your glasses on if you wear them, and pull and pat it into different shapes.

• If you have an oval face, you are very lucky. Any style will suit you.
• A long face is best complemented by short hair that is quite full, with a fringe. Don't go for a severe long hairdo that will only accentuate the length of your face.
• If you have a round face, you should aim to add length. If you don't want long hair, part your hair on the side or add fullness on top. Avoid a neat bob with a fringe.
• All a square face needs is a little softening if the jawline is too heavy. Draw the attention away from the jaw with a diagonal fringe, soft tendrils of hair falling forward from the hairline and around the ears if you wear your hair up, or long loose hair with a bit of bounce below chin level.
• A heart-shaped face is also easy to flatter. All you need to do is avoid a heavy slab of a fringe that will make your face into a triangle. A softer fringe will help.
• Try a soft fringe too for a high forehead, or try a very heavy fridge that starts quite a way back and is 'V'-shaped, with the point of the 'V' in the centre of your forehead.
• If you have a receding or double chin, you need to draw attention away from it. Your hair will look best either piled to the top and back of your head, to balance the chin, or hanging loose to hide it.
• A large nose needs a short, fluffy style — anything sleek or straight will only over-emphasise it.

Once you have decided on the shape of style that will suit your face, you need to look at your hair type and see how the requirements of the one fit the potential of the other. Your hair may be thick or fine, curly or straight, and these factors will determine to a certain extent what you can do with it.

If you have thick or curly hair, you have plenty of natural volume to play with. Fine straight hair needs to be long, or permed, before you can achieve much volume — the sleek look is what comes naturally to you. However, the success of your hairstyle depends on the cut, and this can do much to offset any problems you may have with the nature of your hair.

Choosing a hairdresser

A really good hairdresser is not only an expert stylist — he or she will listen carefully to you, the client, will find out about your lifestyle — whether, for instance, you travel regularly to hot or humid climates or have the leisure to achieve a complicated hairstyle — and above all will look closely at your hair type and condition and advise you on both its potential and its limitations. A top hairdresser whose work you have admired in magazine photographs is not necessarily going to be the right one for you. It may not suit you to have the latest and most outrageous style that he or she has devised for a publicity shot — what you need is personal attention. A good hairdresser is one who will listen to your idea of how you want to look and study photographs of styles you like, and then explain how that style would look on you and also suggest modifications if necessary. A caring hairdresser will try to dissuade you from a drastic change of style or colour that would be wrong for your hair type, besides being expensive and bitterly regretted.

Take your time in settling down with a new hairdresser. A recommendation from a friend may encourage you to visit a new salon, where you can test the waters by having nothing more than a trim and blow-dry. Don't attempt to change your style on the first visit — wait until you're sure that you like the hairdresser's work. A visit to the salon should be a treat, not a chore. Choose somewhere with an atmosphere you like, where the staff are friendly and where the decor and music, if there is any, suit your mood. You want to be relaxed and you want to strike up a rapport with your hairdresser, even if conversation is minimal, otherwise you won't come out looking and feeling your best. It's important that you are punctual — you don't want your stylist to take revenge on your hair — and that if you're kept waiting you get an apology for the delay. Make sure, too, that you choose somewhere where brushes, towels and overalls are absolutely clean. There's nothing less appetising than someone else's dirty comb.

If you have enjoyed your first visit and you look and feel good, you may well have found a winner. Go back for a trim and perhaps a deep-conditioning treatment once a month until you feel confident that your hairdresser understands you and your hair. Only after this trial period should you change your style. Now you'll be looking forward to the results, not dreading them.

A career in hairdressing

Since Vidal Sassoon first appeared on the scene in the 1960s, hairdressing has not only been big business, it has become a field in which personalities achieve stardom and top salons become famous for their individual styling techniques. A successful stylist can make a career on board a luxury liner or travel the world working on photographic sessions for magazines. If you aim to own your own salon, and have an aptitude for stock control, budgeting, advertising and promotion as well as creative styling, there will be openings for you in management.

As in any career, experience is absolutely vital before you can succeed — and in hairdressing it takes a long time to get there. You have to be really dedicated to be willing to stand on the sidelines for so long, sweeping the floor, bringing clients their coffee, shampooing and handing perm papers and scissors to the stylist. But there is a short cut, and this is to go to a hairdressing school. A beginners' course usually lasts about six months and is expensive. Some fees cover a personal set of hairdressing equipment.

The advantages are that you learn faster about every aspect of hairdressing, and though you won't be offered a top job as soon as you have finished your course, you will end up with a diploma that will drastically reduce the time you spend on your apprenticeship. Another point to bear in mind is that hairdressing salons will usually take on only young school leavers, but enrolment in a hairdressing school is not restricted by age, so a six month beginners' course could be your answer if you're looking for a change of career.

In most schools classes are kept small and tuition is intensive. Practical studies take place in salon conditions where cutting, perming, conditioning, colouring and blow-drying are demonstrated on live models. The theory of hair care and hair design, hygiene and salon etiquette are also included in the course — and some schools also run classes on make-up and manicure that can be very useful if you want to diversify.

Hairdressing is a career that you can succeed in wherever you live. It's hard work, but it's creative and it's a job in which you'll be likely to meet a great variety of people. Financial rewards can be high at the top, but wherever you work your greatest reward will be a satisfied client — someone who looks and feels good, thanks to your understanding and skill.

Hair Care at Home

Shampooing

However beautiful your hair is naturally, you need to treat it well, and the first essential is regular shampooing. How often you wash your hair depends entirely on you — wash it as often as you need to keep the scalp scrupulously clean. A mild pH-balanced shampoo correctly formulated for your hair type is best as it won't irritate the scalp or disturb the acid/alkaline balance of the hair. Don't be tempted to use detergents such as washing-up liquid as these will strip the hair of its natural oils. One shampoo will normally suffice. Using warm water from a spray, wet your hair thoroughly. Then pour a little shampoo into your cupped hand and massage it firmly but gently all over your scalp and through your hair. Rinse very thoroughly again from the spray, until the water runs from your hair perfectly free of soap.

In an emergency, you can use a dry shampoo — rub it into the hair and scalp, leave for a minute or two and then brush out — or dab your scalp and hair with cotton wool soaked in eau-de-cologne. Both methods get rid of grease, but of course neither is as satisfactory as a good wash. If you have run out of shampoo, try using the yolks of three eggs, beaten, instead.

Conditioning

There are three basic types of conditioner. A gentle cream moisturises and adds gloss. A rinse gets rid of static and makes hair more manageable. A deep-treatment conditioner nourishes and brings life back to dull or damaged hair. Deep wax or oil treatments should be left on the hair, under plastic film and a towel,

Healthy hair in top condition is your first beauty asset

for as long as possible (overnight is ideal), and used once a week, or once a month, as necessary.

Ordinary conditioners, the creams and rinses, are applied in the same way as shampoo. Massage gently into the scalp and run your fingers through your hair so that it gets to the ends as well as the roots. Leave the conditioner on for a minute or two — perhaps while you soak in the bath or shower — then rinse thoroughly with warm water. A final cool-water rinse flattens the keratin scales on the hair shaft and makes the hair shinier.

You can make a herbal rinse for dark hair by immersing as much rosemary as you can find in water, bringing to the boil and leaving to steep overnight. Strain off the liquid and mix it half and half with cider vinegar. Use diluted with two parts of warm water. For fair or blonde hair, use camomile instead of rosemary.

When you shampoo your hair, be thorough, but gentle. Work the lather in carefully, massaging the scalp with the fingertips. Rinse your hair with lukewarm water from a bathroom hose before conditioning. The tips of your hair, especially if it is long, will need particular attention. Rinse again, and wrap your hair in a towel

Drying

Whatever method you choose for drying your hair, you should first comb it through. Start at the tip, easing the tangles gently out, and work back along the hairshaft. If you start at the scalp, you'll only create fiercer tangles lower down. Take your time and don't tug — carelessness will damage your hair. Use a wide-toothed comb on wet hair — it will free the tangles more easily than a fine-toothed one. Leave your brush (if you use one at all — they often cause static) until your hair is dry. It will snarl wet hair and stretch it to breaking point.

The best way to dry your hair is to leave it and let it dry naturally. To add body and increase the manageability of fine hair, use a mousse or gel. Squirt the mousse or squeeze the gel onto a cupped hand. Rub your palms together, then spread the mousse or gel over the hair. Comb through into the style you want, or comb back from the face to give extra lift. Another way of giv-

Any hairstyle will hold better and last longer if you use a styling aid such as a mousse or gel

ing your hair a lift is to scrunch it up with your fingers as it dries. If you haven't the time to let your hair dry naturally, blot and squeeze dry with a towel before combing out. You can then set or blow dry.

To set, first apply the setting lotion of your choice, then divide your hair with a tail comb into even sections. Don't put too much hair on any one roller. Curly hair will get even curlier on small rollers — use larger ones for a healthy bounce. Thin hair needs to be rolled into a tighter curl on smaller rollers. Hold the hair away from the head at an angle of 90 degrees, and wind firmly, but without stretching, onto the roller. Secure with a pin. Use sellotape or clips for curls around the face. If you don't like the idea of rollers and pins, try the new 'shap-

The model's long fine hair would be damaged by heated rollers and a perm would almost certainly cause it to break. When she wants a curly look the ideal way to achieve it is to use bendy shapers — the modern equivalent of rags. The hair is wrapped round the shapers while still slightly damp, then allowed to dry naturally. Shapers are simple to use. They are made of bendy lightweight foam and to secure them you just twist them over. They come in bright colours and look more decorative than rollers. They are heat resistant, so you can use a blow drier if you wish. When the hair is dry, unwind the shapers and fluff it out with the fingers.

Other ways of creating a curl are with more traditional rollers or with heated styling tongs. When using rollers, be careful not to put too much strain on the hair at the roots. If possible, allow the hair to dry naturally

ers'. They are bendy sticks round which you wind your hair. You then twist the shaper round on itself to hold the hair in place. Shapers act on the same principle as rags did, when they were used to curl Goldilocks-type hair. They are colourful and look pretty, which is more than can be said for rollers, so you won't feel embarrassed if you're interrupted wearing them.

If you set your hair, you should wait until it is completely dry before taking out the rollers. If you are sitting under a dryer, turn it off before your hair is quite dry and let the drying process finish naturally. Excessive heat is always damaging to the hair.

Comb each lock of hair through as you remove the rollers, starting at the nape of the neck and working up to the forehead. If the result is too hard and you can see the partings left by the rollers, you may need a little gentle backbrushing to disguise your handiwork, but be careful not to back-comb or brush too

vigorously, as this will break the hairshaft. A light hairspray applied directly from the aerosol, or sprayed onto a brush and run through the hair if your style is smooth and sleek, will help hold the shape longer.

Most modern styles rely not on a set, but on a superb cut and clever blow-drying. When a hairdresser blow-dries your hair it takes next to no time and looks very simple indeed, but as you will find when you start to do it yourself, it needs a little practice. Choose a plastic wand brush with widely spaced, springy bristles and hold it in your right hand if you are right-handed. Work from the nape, pinning the damp top hair on top of your head out of the way. Divide the hair into sections and wind it over the brush. Blow with the hairdrier from the root to the end of the strands. Don't hold it too close to the hair and keep it moving all the time, always in the direction of the hair growth. Work your way round the sides of your head and finish off with the crown.

Looking After Problem Hair

Oily hair

The result of overactive sebaceous glands is oily hair and skin. Oily hair is most often fine hair, and this aggravates the problem of lank and lifeless locks. You should watch your diet and cut out greasy foods. Plenty of fresh fruit and salads with lots of mineral water to drink will help. It will come as a great relief to you to know that it is a fallacy that frequent shampooing makes the hair even more greasy. If you spent your adolescent years in misery because you were told you should only wash your hair every three days even though it was dreadfully greasy for two of them, then forget it. Your hair looks good only when it is clean, so wash it as often as you like — even twice a day if the weather is hot and sticky or very windy.

Use a mild shampoo and use a cream conditioner only at the ends of long hair. The best after-shampoo rinse for an oily head is an astringent one. Try a home-made herbal rinse or simply dilute some cider vinegar (stronger vinegars will have you smelling like a fish and chip shop) in lukewarm water and sluice it over your head after washing your hair. The acid in it will flatten the keratin scales on the hairshaft and give extra shine as well as counteracting the grease.

Another very useful preparation for oily hair, especially when it is fine and flyaway too, is a hair gel or mousse. Even if you let your hair dry naturally after applying it, you will find it gives extra bounce and texture.

Dry hair

Dry hair is caused by under-active sebaceous glands or by over-exposure to wind, salt or chlorinated water or heat. Heat is the most common source of damage to the hair, whether from the sun, over-use of the hairdryer or heated styling appliances, or from central heating. Too frequent perming and bleaching also makes the hair brittle and unmanageable. If your hair has a constant tendency to break, apparently for none of these reasons, check with your doctor, as it may be due to drugs you are being prescribed.

Washing dry hair will not strip it of its natural oils, as it used to be thought. Whatever your hair type, your prime objective must be to keep it clean and if you use the correct products gently massaged into the scalp you will be able to restore shine to the driest hair. Use a rich shampoo, rinse clean with lukewarm water and follow with a cream conditioner, combing it through to the ends of the hair. Once a week, give yourself a warm olive oil or wax treatment. Massage it well into the scalp, comb the hair through and cover in cling film, then wrap in a towel or scarf. Leave it on for at least an hour, or overnight if you can. Wash out the oil with two latherings of shampoo and condition as normal. This treatment is especially good for bleached or heat-damaged hair.

Dandruff

The best treatment for dandruff is frequent shampooing with a mild shampoo. For a severe case of dandruff use a medicated shampoo. The most important thing is to keep the scalp scrupulously clean. Make sure that your diet is a healthy one and includes white meat or fish, eggs, cheese, fresh fruit and raw vegetables. Drink plenty of mineral water. Take exercise to help overcome tension. If dandruff persists, visit your doctor.

Excessive hair loss

Normally about 50 hairs will be lost from the head each

A regular deep-conditioning treatment is necessary to nourish dry hair and keep it glossy.

Condition your hair after every shampoo and deep-condition once a month

Long hair should be treated with the utmost care — avoid chemicals and heated appliances if you can. Pay special attention to the tips, which can be as much as six years old. Condition them and get them trimmed regularly to avoid unsightly split ends

day. If your hair loss is more severe, the first thing to do is check your diet. Your hair will never be luxuriant if your diet is poor. Try to get plenty of fresh air and exercise, as well as lots of sleep. Use a comb, not a brush. Slightly more hair loss in spring and autumn is quite natural. Keep your hair short

— it will look fuller and the weight of long hair may cause more of it to fall out. See your doctor or trichologist if you are upset by this problem.

Split and broken hair

If your hair is in very bad condition, splitting and breaking, it can be due to over-perming and bleaching, or to careless use of heated styling appliances or severe exposure to a merciless sun. Breaks and splits can never be mended, so your hair will need a good professional cut and regular trimming until new growth has replaced the damaged hair. In the meantime, treat your hair gently and give it a weekly deep-conditioning treatment to restore its shine. If you wish to perm or colour your hair yourself at this stage, take care to follow the manufacturer's instructions. If, when your hair is in better condition, you decide to perm or colour it professionally, always get your hairdresser to do a strand test first.

Keeping it long

Long hair is a valuable asset and needs to be treated very gently. If you are contemplating a change of colour, or a perm, always take your hairdresser's advice and don't attempt anything drastic at home.

To keep long hair in top condition and avoid broken and split ends, you will need to be aware that your number one enemy is heat. The tips of your hair are probably about four years old, and four years of regular treatment with hairdryers and various electrical styling appliances may often result in some damage. The ends of long hair should be trimmed regularly to remove split ends, and your hair should be allowed to dry naturally if possible. If you want to add bounce or curl without endangering your hair by constant use of heated rollers, try using bending shapers, or, if you can't find these in the shops, use the old-fashioned rag technique. Both work on the same principle — used on slightly damp hair they will

give plenty of movement, while on dry hair they will give bounce. They are particularly effective when used in conjunction with a styling mousse. When you dress out the hair, finger the curls apart, starting from the nape and sides of the head and finishing with the crown. Brush through for a fluffier style.

More time-consuming, but very spectacular, is the pre-Raphaelite look. This is achieved by making tiny plaits — as many as you can manage — all over the head. It is best done on damp hair and left overnight. In the morning, undo the plaits and carefully finger through. Be sparing with your brush and comb if you want to keep the gently rippling curls in longer.

If you are prepared to spend some time perfecting your techniques with plaits, knots, buns and chignons, you can create a whole wardrobe of styles that will change your appearance as dramatically as a new outfit, but cost you next to nothing. Start with a simple pony tail, making sure that you always use a covered elastic band and remove it gently, and coil the hair this way and that to see what suits you. Enlist the aid of a few stylish combs and slides, and buy yourself a collection of pretty ribbons.

You may decide to adopt a new and sophisticated style for a special occasion. Experiment with it first! Don't leave it to the last minute: you may find it doesn't suit you at all, or that you feel self-conscious and unused to your new image — or even that your friends don't recognise you!

If the special occasion is your own wedding, then it's vital that you have a trial run. Your hairdresser will want to know the style of your dress, and headdress, if you are wearing one. Take your headdress along with you so that your hairdresser can show you how to secure it — the last thing you want on your wedding day is a hairstyle collapsing under the weight of yards of lace, or a veil that takes off at the slightest gust of wind.

Black Afro hair

The range of beauty products for black hair and the number of hairdressers who specialise in Afro styling has increased dramatically over the past 10 years. As with any other hair type, a balanced diet is needed for healthy hair, but black hair has extra requirements because it is coarse, fragile and dry and highly susceptible to atmospheric conditions.

Not so long ago, the answer to brittle, dull and unmanageable black hair used to be a thick coating of oil applied after infrequent washing. It was supposed to act as a straightener and a gloss. It had to be removed with a strong detergent shampoo as it clogged the hair follicles. The shampoo stripped the hair, undoing any good the oil might have done it, and irritated the scalp into the bargain. Hair loss and dandruff were often the results. Today's preparations are lighter and kinder to the hair and leave it looking clean and healthy.

Black hair should be washed as often as necessary with a mild shampoo. Always follow the shampoo with a conditioner, and give your hair a wax or oil deep-conditioning treatment every month or fortnight. For dry or irritated scalps there are special scalp conditioners. Moisturise your hair every day you don't wash it with one of the aerosol preparations available at your chemist. Because black hair is so sensitive to atmosphere and will lose moisture rapidly when it is dry and hot, and absorb moisture in damp conditions, so losing its style, you may find a reversion-resistant hair spray is a help. This will both hold your style and prevent excess loss of precious moisture — but use it sparingly to avoid a rigid look.

Get your hair trimmed regularly — black hair is wayward and needs constant taming as well as pampering. Many black women who don't like the limitations of the frizzy halo now sculpt their hair in a spectacular design of head-plaits.

HAIR BY TREVOR SORBIE

Hair has been coloured a warm dark brown and styled with mousse for a soft curl. Brushed up and back from the face to give body and fullness, the mane-shaped style is held in place with a row of tiny bows

Just an illusion — this style has been created with the clever use of hairpieces — a stunning way of changing your looks without growing your hair long

This naturally curly hair is tinted arctic blonde above the temples and low-lighted for curl definition. The airy top is complimented by cropped sides and back for a triangular silhouette, defying the round head shape that holds most wearers of curly hair

HAIR BY DON MIKULA FOR VIDAL ASSOON

Naturally curly hair has been straightened and tong-set for a fuller more bouyant curl. The auburn highlights follow the gentle upward movement of the front hair, while the back and sides are cropped short to create a neat head shape

This can be the most individual expression of your personality — it can be the height of elegance, intricately coiled and corn-rowed, or it can be a simple fringe of tiny plaits framing your face.

Another way to tame black hair is to straighten it. If you are wary of the damaging potential of chemical straightening on fragile hair, you can use a hot comb or curling tongs. The hair will need to be well conditioned before heat is applied. After washing, divide your hair into five sections — top, two sides, crown and nape. Twist and pin up each section out of the way. Beginning at the nape, apply concentrated scalp and hair conditioner. Comb a layer of the hair downwards, rub conditioner into the scalp with the fingertips, and comb it right through the hair, paying special attention to the ends. Gradually move round the sides and front of the head, finishing with the crown. It is a process that will take time, but the end result — glossy, well protected hair — will be well worth the effort.

Once the whole head has been conditioned, you can begin to go over the hair again, smoothing it out with the curling tongs or hot comb. Always use an appliance that is thermostatically controlled. When you have worked through each section and all the hair is straight, curl the hair into style on large rollers, or with the curling tongs.

For information on chemical straightening and a new soft curly perm for black hair, see the section on perming and straightening. If you want to colour your hair, you should seek the advice of a professional hairdresser. It is difficult to colour very curly hair yourself and harsh chemicals are not kind to dry, brittle hair or sensitive scalps. A semi-permanent rinse in a rich chestnut or deep brown can add depth and glow to your hair colour, and spray-on highlights and glitter look stunning for a temporary change of mood.

HAIR CLAIROL

Colouring Your Hair

There are three different types of hair colour: temporary, semi-permanent and permanent.

Temporary colour

The mildest colourant you can use is the water rinse. This adds colour to the outer layer of the hair, the cuticle, which is then washed away with the next shampoo. It will also come off, of course, if you go out in the rain. Water rinses are useful to tone streaks of grey hair or to soften a too-brassy blond. Usually, no skin test is needed for water rinses. They are simple to use at home and usually applied after shampooing. The same effects can be achieved with coloured setting lotions, all-in-one shampoo/rinses, coloured sprays, gels or mousses.

Semi-permanent colour

Semi-permanents contain no bleaching agents and so cannot lighten the hair — they merely change its tone. The colour does penetrate the cuticle temporarily, but is washed out after about half a dozen shampoos. A semi-permanent tint is useful for disguising grey hairs, giving depth to mousy hair and life to a dull blonde, or enriching brown hair with reddish tones. If you tint your hair at home, you will need to carry out a skin test 24 hours before you use the product on your hair. If you follow the manufacturer's instructions closely, you will give your hair added lustre as well as colour, because most contain an effective conditioner.

Permanent colour

Using a permanent tint is the only way to change your hair colour drastically. Exercise restraint if you want the results to look natural, and choose a tint that's only two or three shades lighter than your own colour. A strand test will help you decide if you've made the right choice. Don't chop a great chunk out of your hair for

this — take about 50 hairs (which is after all only one day's natural hair loss) from all over your head. Follow the manufacturer's instructions and study the results in the sunlight. If you like what you see, hold the strand to your face and check that it doesn't clash with your complexion. Permanent tints are mixed with hydrogen peroxide and you

should always carry out a skin test 24 hours in advance of using the product on your hair. If you are colouring your own hair, a good place to test the tint is on the tender skin inside the forearm. A hairdresser will normally do the test behind your ear, where it won't show if your skin reacts badly, but you need to do it somewhere where you can see it. Make sure not to wash the patch of skin you have tested, and if the product irritates your skin at all, don't use it.

Permanent tinting is a chemical process that works by lifting the overlapping keratin cells on the cuticle and penetrating the hairshaft. The bleach strips the hair of its natural colour and makes the cortex porous. The cortex then absorbs the new colour. Timing is crucial, and a professional colorist will be best able

Imaginative colouring and styling have created this stunning effect. Two colours — red and white — have been applied to the hair. This has been repeated throughout the hair. The finished effect complements the cut and results in a superb dappled look

A hair colouring technique has been used to achieve a subtle blend of colour throughout the crown and forehead area. There is no methodical approach with this technique. Colour only as much hair as you feel emphasises the hair style. With this style the nape and the sides were left untreated to achieve a three-dimensional effect

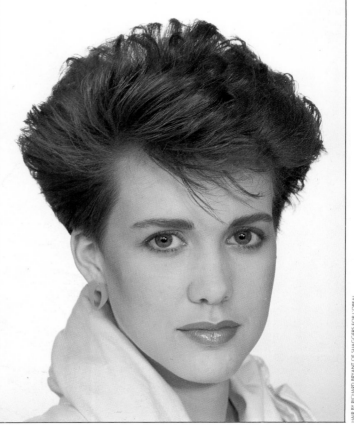

Using tin foil, three colours are applied to sections of the hair

Each time a different colour order is used — white, red and black, the red, white and black, then black, white and red

The foil is then wrapped firmly around the model's hair. The finished effect (right) is a unique marbling effect

HAIR CUT BY VIDAL SASSOON

to judge how long to leave the colour on your particular hair type — finer hair takes less time to absorb the colour than coarser hair. Permanent tinting can go badly wrong, resulting in a surprising colour and damaged hair, if it is not done properly. If you choose to do it at home, make sure you follow the manufacturer's instructions exactly. Misuse of bleaching or permanent colouring may cause your hair to split and break. Your hairdresser may advise you to try a gentler method until your permanent colour has grown out.

Highlighting, streaking and tipping are sophisticated and selective forms of permanent colouring that require expert timing and blending. Nowadays they can be carried out at home. Professional highlighting is popular, though expensive, because it emphasises the nuances of colour in your hair, underlining its natural beauty. Strands of hair are drawn through holes in a plastic cap and treated with bleach or woven out and then wrapped in tin foil. The bleach is rinsed off when the desired colour has been reached, then the whole head is shampooed and conditioned, perhaps after having been treated with a semi-permanent toner to blend the shades more subtly. Highlights grow out fairly naturally and need to be renewed only every three or four months.

In another process, bleach is painted in narrow stripes down the length of the hair. If you attempt this at home, you may end up looking like a zebra.

Tipping is exactly what it says — colouring just the ends of the hair. Often two or three shades of colour are used in all of these processes.

Vegetable dyes
Unlike chemical dyes these do not alter the structure of your hair. They are non-toxic, so no skin test is necessary. Vegetable dyes cling to the cuticle of the hair and leave it soft, shining and full of body —

so they are particularly useful on fine limp hair.

The most popular vegetable dye is henna, which has been used for thousands of years to give the hair rich red tones. There are different shades of henna available today — some of them compounded with other substances — and these are not compatible with any form of permanent hair colour or permanent wave. Always do a strand test, though the instruction leaflets that come with most brands of true red henna usually err on the cautious side where timing is concerned — in eastern countries women leave henna on their heads for 48 hours, basting occasionally with oil to stop it drying out.

Henna is the dried crushed leaves of the plant *Lawsonia alba*. It is mixed with hot water and a dash of lemon juice or vinegar and, for the most even results, painted onto the hair section by section. If you do this at home you will be bound to make a mess. Wear old clothes and be prepared to spend some time cleaning your bathroom afterwards. Pile the hennaed hair on top of your head, cleaning any henna off your skin with damp cotton wool (pay attention to the ears, too). Wrap a strip of cotton wool around the hairline to stop the dye running down your face and cover the head in cling film. Tie an old scarf or towel round your head. To speed up the colouring process, warm your head by using a hairdrier or sitting in the sun. When you decide your time is up, wash out the henna with several shampoos and rinse thoroughly with a bathroom spray. Your hair will be left in top condition, full and lustrous. Don't use henna on blonde, grey, white or chemically tinted hair, as the results will be unpredictable.

Other natural dyes can be made from infusions of camomile or marigold, both of which produce a subtle lightening effect, or from sage or walnut, which will give a soft brown tone to grey hair. Walnuts, if you use them, should be boiled for several hours.

Divide the hair into two large sections from ear to ear and secure with clips

Take your first section diagonally on the hairline behind the ear

Alternate the colouring method: 1 Weave out and colour middle lengths; 2 Weave out and colour from

roots to tips; 3 Colour from roots to tips; 4 Colour entire section from roots to tips, working up to crown

Complete the other side in the same way. Work up to join the crown on the back section

Divide the front into five sections back from hairline. Alternate the weave pattern as above

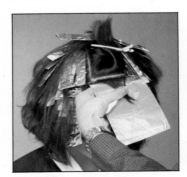

Take the next section above it and work backwards following the same method

Finish with the top section, following the same method alternating the weave to give the result opposite

Reflective Lights

HAIR BY PAUL NATH OF HEADLINE HAIR STUDIO

The two girls on these pages have had their hair tinted and highlighted by the method shown above right. Both styles show the advantage of highlighting to emphasise the movement of the hair, whether it is a soft easy curl or a more scrunched look

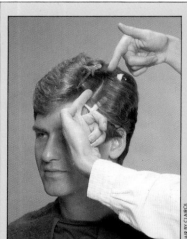

HAIR BY CLAIROL

HAIR BY CLAIROL

the roots of the hair. This will help protect the hair that is to remain untreated as it will lift it off the section that has just been lightened. The colourist works up to the parting, then repeats the process on the other side of the head, first working on the hairline section, then on the horizontal sections on the side and top of the head

The colour is applied with a wide-toothed tinting comb. It is combed through the first section, which is taken parallel to the front hairline and 5mm into it from the parting. The colour is combed straight through from the root to point. The next sections are taken parallel to the parting, about half way down the head. After the colour is combed on, a small strip of cotton wool is placed at

1 Before. To add more texture and colour to fine, light brown hair, thin highlights will be put through, using the weave/Easi-meche technique

2 Take a fine section of hair, weave out strands and, after peeling back the clear sheet, place the opaque side underneath (as close to the roots as possible). Stick hair to the blue adhesive strip, which will hold it in place

3 Mix Platin Eclair with 30-volume oxidant and apply to hair from just above the dark blue adhesive strip. Place edge of clear sheet slightly above blue line and seal in a downwards movement at edges only

4 After the whole head has been highlighted, leave to develop for 35 minutes (you can see at a glance how the colour is taking because of the clear top sheet). Shampoo, then condition hair

Perming

Today's perms aim not for a rigid waffle-iron effect but for softness, bounce, volume and movement. They are especially useful for fine straight hair that lacks body. If you covet a tight curl you can still have it, but without dryness, frizz and breaking hairs. There is also a new curly perm for black hair that brings softness and regularity to wayward and wiry curls.

Modern perms, used properly, should leave your hair shining and lustrous, but perming is nevertheless a chemical process that alters the structure of the hair and is therefore potentially damaging to it. Because of the necessity for exact timing and correct choice of perming solution — it comes in varying strengths — it is wise to go to a salon instead of attempting to perm your hair at home. If you do perm your own hair, make sure you follow the manufacturer's instructions to the letter.

The perm is a two-stage process. The first lotion applied is a chemical that softens the structure of the hair; this is then rinsed away very thoroughly and the second lotion is applied. This is a neutraliser that sets the hair into the new position determined by the curling rods. A final rinse and the perm is complete.

You should not perm damaged hair. Don't perm and tint within the same two weeks, and don't perm if you have an irritated scalp. Always take great care of permed hair, using a conditioner each time you wash. Avoid brushing if possible, as this will pull out the curl. If you have a wash-and-wear curly style, try to let your hair dry naturally and run your fingers through it as it dries for a soft bouncy look. Use a wide- not a narrow-toothed comb. If your hair looks a bit squashed after you've slept on it, spray it with water from a plant spray and it will spring into shape.

Straightening

This is a very drastic process, and very different from perming. The structure of the hair is altered, but the hairshaft is stretched before being set into its new shape — and this is where the damage is likely to occur because hair breaks very easily if it is stretched when wet. Because black hair is by nature brittle and porous, straightening should be carried out only in a salon. Remember that as new curly hair grows the straightened hair will look less natural — perming is a more successful process as the weight of the hair as it grows softens the curl.

This natural looking perm has given body to fine hair. Scrunch drying with gel creates a carefree tousled look

A softly curled perm for a sophisticated look. The perm has given height and fullness to shoulder-length, layer-cut hair. Highlights emphasise the bounce of the curl

The model's long hair has been given a curly perm. It is layer-cut for easy manageability and to give a tapered rather than a pyramid shape. The curls are teased out for a fluffy corkscrew effect

This pyramid cut shows off the abundance of the model's pre-Raphaelite perm, and her hair has been tinted the golden red traditional for the style

The model's straight hair is in top condition. To give it lift and interest, she chooses light gold highlights and a loose shaggy curl. The result is sultry and sophisticated (right).

Chapter 6

Hair Styles

The model's thick medium-length hair was layer cut, lightly permed and then trimmed again to give it a natural exuberance. The curls escape in confusion from their jaunty ribbon for a look that's both sporty and glamorous. An example of how an untamed hairstyle can complement a demurely youthful face

Another untamed look this time combined with the formal elegance of diamante chandelier earrings, a plunge-necked dress and sophisticated make-up, to create a sultry evening look. The model's hair has been softly feathered around the face, but remains full and heavy at the back. The highlights emphasise the movement of the hair. A good dramatic style that needs a minimum of looking after

A longer, fluffier version of the urchin look — a sort of punk Elizabeth Taylor. The feathery cut has been given a lift with a light bouncy perm. Styling mousse combined with scrunch drying results in a carefree windblown style

This haircut was created by triangle sectioning to achieve a very natural look. The colour was painted on, using the tri-light technique, to underline the fall and swing of the style. Use a mousse or gel and a light hairspray to keep this style in shape

69

Soft fine hair cut at jaw level is given shine and manageability with mousse. The hair has been finger-dried for maximum textures and highlights accentuate its gentle movement

Fine hair has been given a light perm and finger-dried with gel for this romantic look that accentuates the model's impish features. An easy-to-care-for style on a soft blonde tint

HAIR BY STEVIE BUCKLE SALON

HAIR L'OREAL

Another style on the same hair as top left, but this time smoother and more sophisticated. The model's hair has been deep-conditioned after subtle highlighting. Blow drying completes the natural effect

The same model and a third style, showing the versatility of a superb jaw-level cut. Blow drying combined with hair gel gives her fine hair body and fullness and a carefree sophisticated style that will take her through the day

HAIR L'OREAL

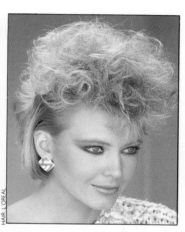

HAIR L'OREAL

A slightly longer style with plenty of froth on top, achieved by scrunch drying on hair gel. The airy curls enhance the golden tint of the hair and the sleeked-down sides give the model's face added height

Short fine hair with a smoother look. Softly upwards-brushed, this style is both simple and elegant. The model's cool make-up reflects her poise

USING STYLING MOUSSE

1 When you have washed and conditioned your hair, squeeze it gently in a towel, then comb or finger through. Fingers are best for permed hair like the model's, but if you use a comb, choose a wide-toothed one. Shake the aerosol can of styling mousse and squirt some into the palm of your hand

2 Taking a little mousse at a time, scrunch it into your hair until you have covered your whole head evenly, from tips to roots

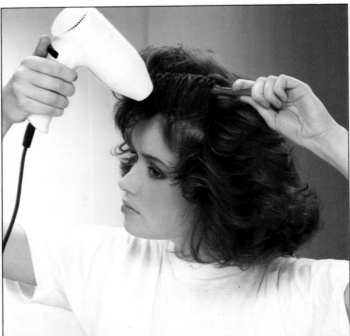

3 Now you are ready to scrunch dry your hair, using a hairdrier for speed. Don't hold the drier too close to your head. Take a handful of hair and squeeze it together, lifting at the roots. Point the drier at it in an upwards angle. Carry on doing this all over your head until your hair is dry

4 The alternative method, which gives you greater control, but looks just as natural, is to blow dry with a brush. Starting at the nape of the neck, roll the hair round the brush and lift at the roots. Aim the drier at the roots and follow along the hair shaft. Continue this process, working round the sides of the head to the top, and finish with the crown

The finished look is a carefree mass of light curls that should stay bouyant all day. Setting mousses leave your hair soft and shining naturally

A pert upswept style for softly permed hair set with gel

HAIR: SHERMAN PERU

Long hair formed into a soft French pleat with a wild profusion of curls on top teased out to balloon spectacularly forward

HAIR: STEVIE BUCKLE

HAIR: SCHUMI

The mid-length shaggy cut has the ends of the hair slivered and frayed with scissors and a razor. The roots are then permed leaving the tips completely untouched. Setting mousse is applied and the hair is rough dried for a savage look

A soft look for fine hair that's cut to just below ear level. Blow drying creates fullness, and highlighting emphasises the movement of the hair

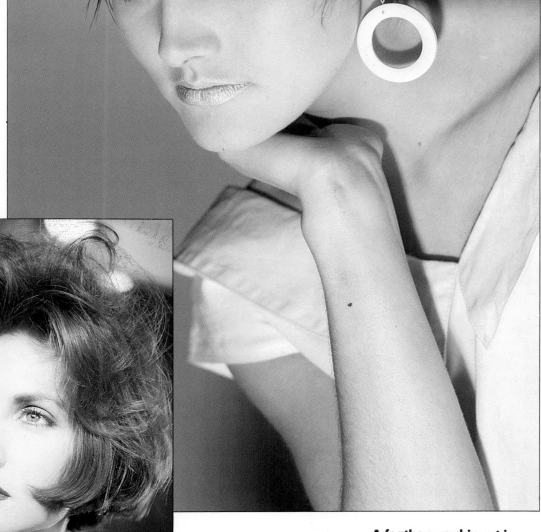

HAIR: STEVIE BUCKLE SALON

HAIR: STEVIE BUCKLE SALON

A feathery urchin cut is given positive shape by blow drying with hair gel. Cropped really short at the back and left soft and full on top, this is an ideal style for fine hair

EXPERT CUTTING

1 Straight, lifeless hair is transformed into a frothy extrovert layered style in the hands of an expert. A centre parting is taken from the front of the forehead to the nape of the neck and a straight guideline is cut at the back. The back hair is levelled to this guideline, by working in small sections up to the crown of the head

2 Then the hairdresser starts on the sides, taking a diagonal section from the front through to the nape of the neck. The fringe is cut by working forward to the temples, where the hair is moved forward and cut at a steeper angle, so that the line of the hair curves slightly at the front

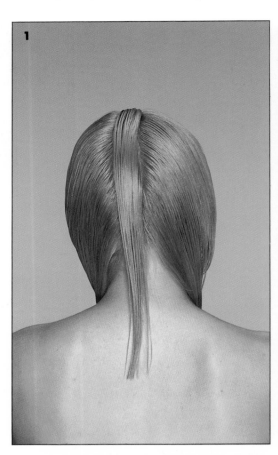

3 Cutting in the same way, the stylist continues up to the centre parting. The same process is repeated on the other side of the head, starting at the crown and working through to the forehead

4 The top of the hair is lifted at 90 degrees to the head and cut about 5 cm (2½ inches) long, keeping it parallel to the horizontal. The same process is repeated on the other side of the head, starting at the crown and working through to the forehead

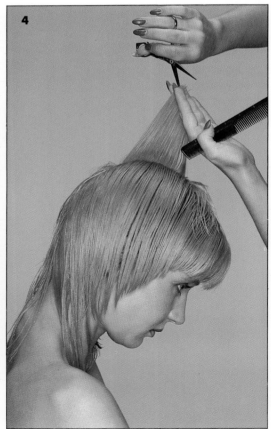

76

6 For the finished look, the hair is blow dried with mousse to create a style that's full and soft, bouncy and feathery. The hair is swept out at the sides to emphasise the model's almond eyes, and left long behind the ears to accentuate her high cheekbones and full mouth

5 The side hair is cut by combing the hair up and over the head and cutting upwards from the nape to the crown in small sections, following the first section of hair as a guideline. The process is repeated on the other side, before the hair is checked for even cutting in horizontal sections from ear to ear across the crown

A bouffant layered look styled with rollers or heated tongs. The hair is lifted and gently fronded — a feathery look always softens and flatters features that tend to be heavy (left)

Tousled short hair spiked with highlights gives the model a kittenish look that teams surprisingly well with her sophisticated jewellery and make-up (right)

This fringed crop, neatly cut into the nape of the neck and left longer and softer on top, is highlighted to stress its bouyant movement. An easy style as long as it's kept trimmed — all you need to do is wash and scrunch dry with hair gel (top left)

Triangle sectioning with layered top and sides creates this short textured bob. The warm and natural colour effect is achieved with three different shades of highlighting (right)

A light perm and scrunch drying give medium-short hair the sultry schoolgirl look. Understate it with natural make-up and a shirt and tie (below)

HAIR BY TREVOR SORBIE

HAIR BY OSSIE RIZZO — SANRIZZ

A good cut on hair that's in superb condition. This tousled style needs only a blow dry or a scrunch dry to make it look its best. Ideal for a busy or sporty life, it's a cut that will suit hair of a fine or medium texture (above)

For the best results, this jaw-length style should be blow dried, to create maximum fullness at the back. The soft, flyaway shape complements the model's neat features (below)

Short fluffy style with bounce on top that fronds forward softly and slims a full face. A gentle styling mousse will help the hair stay as you want it — use curling tongs to create the loop effect on top (above)

A classic backswept bob suits this model's well-balanced features and her medium-weight hair. Anyone with a pretty hair line should show it off. The secret with this style is a good cut and hair in perfect condition

A neo-punk look with fullness at the back at mid-ear level. The top hair can be made spikier, if you feel so inclined, with hair gel. This soft look suits a more sophisticated occasion

HAIR BY JAMES LEBON AT CUTS COMPANY

HAIR BY AVRAM FOR VIDAL SASSOON

HAIR BY CARMEL AT CLIFFORD STAFFORD

The model's abundant dark hair was heavy and flat. A short cut and a soft curly perm give her a carefree wayward look accentuated by the soft fringing around the face. A semi- permanent rinse brought back the gloss and shine of health to her hair (above)

HAIR BY MARIO OF MICHAELJOHN FOR WELLA

HAIR BY CARMEL AT CLIFFORD STAFFORD

HAIR BY CARMEL AT CLIFFORD STAFFORD

A simple blow-dry style that sweeps back from the model's face and falls gently to the right, detracting from a low forehead. The rather fine hair is given fullness and boost with the addition of highlights. Light blonde and warm peach give interest to mousy hair (above)

The model's hair was long and straight — but she was tired of looking demure. As she wanted to keep her hair long and in good condition, she was advised against a perm and permanent hair colour — instead the hair was gently layered on top and styled with heated rollers to give height. The upsweep over the ears is emphasised with painted highlights of pink and blonde (left)

The model's natural reddish tones have been heightened to a bright and lustrous copper that perfectly suits her pale complexion. The tousled style emphasises the glorious colour and shine of her hair and she needs only the minimum of make-up to complete this natural look (above right)

You can wear your hair 'up' even if it's only jaw length with this tousled style. Heated rollers give the hair its shape, curving up over the crown from left to right. Gentle back-combing makes the hair frothy on top — but the most important ingredient in this style is the highlighting, which accentuates the movement of the hair (right)

The model's abundant long hair has been layer cut then roller-set. Backbrushing creates a full lion's mane effect that emphasises the delicacy of her features in a stunning evening style

This soft brush-swept style depends on a superb cut. It is lightly permed, then set on large rollers to give plenty of swirling movement (below right)

The straight chop is a simple cut that has had spectacular things done to it. Highlights and spiky drying with hair gel create a look that's both sophisticated and savage (below)

Permed hair has been finger-dried with hair gel to give a light and fluffy haloed effect (above)

This short curly perm is given a sculpted look with plenty of height on top by being brushed back severely from the face at the sides and set with gel. The top is teased out and the back upswept, giving the illusion of long hair

An easy-to-live-with classic style. A curly perm on mid-length hair cut to a soft halo for bounce and fullness (below)

Two ways with the same cut — a curly, casual style for day wear suits the model's outgoing personality. For evening, skilful blow drying transforms her tousled locks into a sleek, sophisticated and artfully sculpted style. An expert cut on thick curly hair gives amazing versatility

The model's fine straight hair has been wet-set with rollers for evening wear. Brushed up dramatically at the sides, it escapes from its rigid outline in a wispy coif over the forehead. Pink streaks lend an air of frivolity to this original look

This classic bob is a beautiful easy-to-manage style for straight heavy hair that is shining with health. It needs expert and regular trimming to keep its clearly defined geometrical shape. The wearer will always look and feel immaculate

The model's fine soft hair droops limply around her face. She is transformed with an unusual style called the swan line. The hair is lifted up and away from the face at the sides and back in graceful curves, giving otherwise lifeless hair plenty of texture and movement. The style is held in place with gel and a gentle spray and shows off the model's delicate features

The same model and cut as below right — but this time the hair has been roller-set for a smooth and sophisticated outline. Brushed up and back from the face and down neatly into the nape, this style shows how versatile a good cut can be

Simple elegance. The hair is cut short at the sides and into the nape of the neck, and left longer on top to create height and fullness. It is tong-set backwards with gel, and highlights accentuate the soft curl (below right)

Lightly layered hair is given the shaggy look by being scrunch dried with gel. The highlights accentuate the wildness and movement of the style

A shaggy cut on heavier hair that has been scrunch dried with gel. The hair is allowed to tangle over the forehead, creating a savage jungle look

HAIR BY BEVERLY HILLS TRAMPP

A profusion of curls created by scrunch drying on gel — a style to give lift and fullness to fine hair. The hair has been lightened and highlighted to give extra softness

HAIR BY DANIEL GAVIN

HAIR BY SCHUMI

The shingle. The heavy fringe and side hair are given a surprise ending with a feathered edge that fronds forward onto the cheeks. The back is tapered neatly into the nape

A short cut that needs very little attention — in fact it can be combed into shape and simply left to dry. Layer-cut for fullness on the top, it is cropped over the ears but left longer at the back to curl jauntily round beneath them

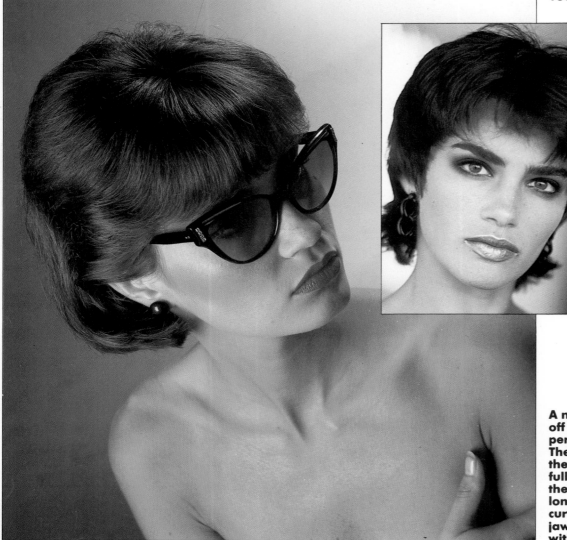

HAIR BY SCHUMI

HAIRCUT VIDAL SASSOON

A neat helmet shape shows off the shine of the model's perfectly conditioned hair. The top hair springs from the centre of the head in a full-fringed bob, but over the ears the hair is left longer and brushed back, curling under at the jawline. A classic cut, dried with mousse

An unusual cut with the top hair left long and sleeked back and the hair above the ears cut very short for a raised sideburn effect. Black hair has been streaked with red for a dramatic look

HAIR BY ANDI FOR ANTENNA

A long shaggy cut that can be finger lifted as it dries. Use gel to create body and fullness. Highlights add texture and interest

HAIRCUT VIDAL SASSOON

A sophisticated look for evening on shoulder-length hair. The side hair is taken smoothly back and the top hair lifted up and slightly to the side, where it is secured in the centre of the head. A sleek style to show off hair in good condition

HAIR BY SAM McKNIGHT

An easy style for fine hair, cut short at the sides with fullness on top. Highlights add interest. Apply hair gel and scrunch dry the hair to create maximum movement

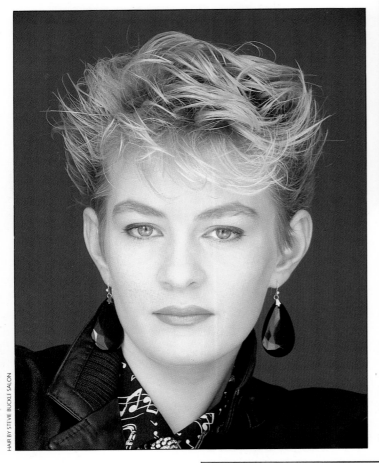

Curly hair can look sleek with the application of a modern hair oil. The hair is cut very short and combed back from the face for a cool svelte style that will take you anywhere — beach, office or nightspot

This avant garde look, reminiscent of Bowie, is achieved with hair gel. The longer hair is slicked back into a ponytail and the shorter front hair brushed up into a bushy coif

The sides have been cut in triangular sections as a more elegant alternative to sideburns. The front hair is left textured and the back cropped close to the head, allowing for a soft and wispy outline, for a look of stunning simplicity. The style is held in place with oil hair mousse

A smooth sophisticated style that gives body to fine hair. The hair is wet-set then brushed up and back over the ears. A wispy fringe can be pulled forward to soften the effect

HAIR CLAIROL

HAIR OSSIE RIZZO AT SANRIZZ

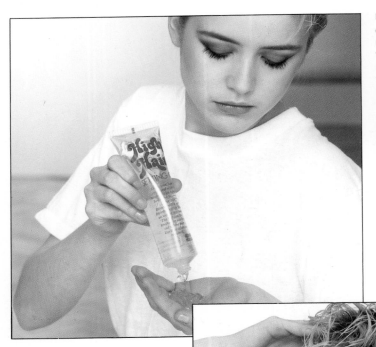

USING HAIR GEL Hair gel allows you to create a more dramatic style than you can achieve with mousse. You can make your hair stand up and do spectacular tricks. It is especially good for creating a spiky, punky look. First, squib some gel into the palm of your hand

The finished look is as prickly as a thistle, but though your hair is literally standing on end, it doesn't feel hard or sticky. Styling gel gives you amazing versatility, particularly if you have fine hair that tends to hang limp and flat (right)

Rub your palms together so the gel covers both hands evenly. Now knead the gel into your hair with a shampooing action, making sure it coats both tips and roots. If you have long hair, you will need to comb the gel right through the hair to make sure it is evenly distributed

To create this style, start with the hair at the sides of the head, combing it up in a wide arc over the ears, and following the line of the comb with the dryer. To create a spiky look on top, finger through the hair in an upward motion, pulling it gently into stiff peaks. Dry from the roots to the tips

The back of the sunray crop is blunt cut below the ear level, but graded highlights add interest and texture. The comb effect of the front of the hair is visible above the smooth-lying back hair

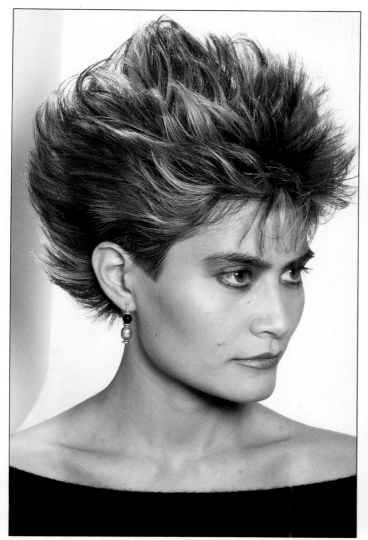

A dramatic punkish style lifted up from the head in flame-like waves. The movement of the hair is emphasised with highlights in three tones and the style is achieved by blow drying on gel

A tough street look with the hair shaved mohican-style above the ears and left long on top to be slicked back with oil mousse (above)

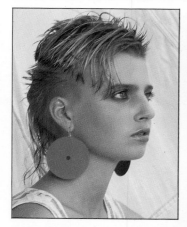

A wet look for summer. The top hair is left fairly long and brushed over to one side with hair gel. The side hair is cropped very short and left fine and natural. Tendrils of hair hang down the nape to complement the top hair

The swan line with extra fullness at the back balances the model's pointed chin and gives life and texture to fine limp hair (left)

The model's fine hair has been cleverly cut to accentuate the urchin quality of her features. This is a style that's fresh and easy to care for. Highlights draw attention to the soft backwards-sweep of the front hair, while the back is neatly trimmed into the nape

Another soft style for fine hair, this time falling in feathery fronds onto the model's face. The hair has been expertly layer cut from the crown to give bounce and highlights add texture. A perfect, easy-care summer style

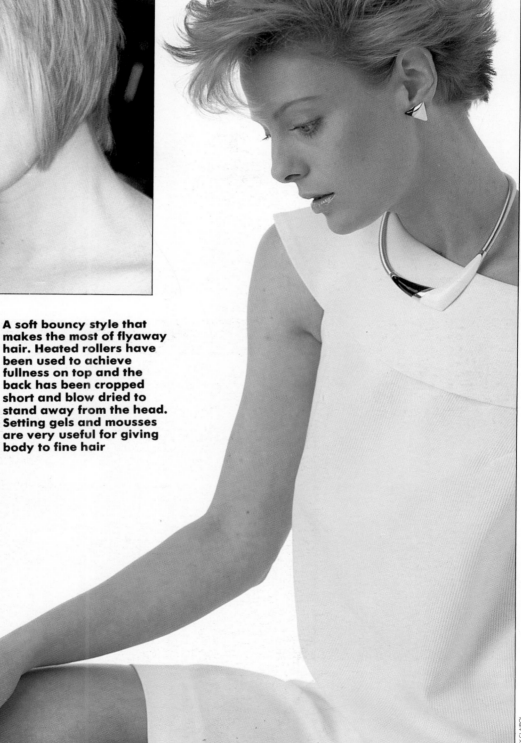

A soft bouncy style that makes the most of flyaway hair. Heated rollers have been used to achieve fullness on top and the back has been cropped short and blow dried to stand away from the head. Setting gels and mousses are very useful for giving body to fine hair

Fine hair always relies on a good cut. Here baby-soft hair falls forward to create a delicate frame for the face. The gentle curl under the jaw draws the attention away from the heavy jawline to the neatly pointed chin (top)

A windswept layered look whose boyishness is emphasised with highlights. The hair is cleverly cut into the nape to give extra height at the crown, accentuating the model's pert jawline and chin (above)

A stunning look achieved with an unusual cutting technique. The hair is cropped very short except at the front, where longer strands have been left amongst the shorter ones to create a softer effect. Two tones of colouring have been used: a stark tangerine on the shorter hair and a lighter gold-blonde on the longer strands (below)

A severe masculine brushcut. The golden-tinted hair has been permed and cleverly cropped. Brushed away from the face, this style is the perfect answer to thick unmanageable hair (right)

HAIR: OSSIE RIZZO AT SANRIZZ

HAIR: TREVOR SORBIE

HAIR: DANIEL GALVIN

A golden sun-god look. A curly perm has been washed and fingered through to give shape to a triangular haloed haircut with ragged natural edges. The breadth at the side above the ears balances a long face and a high forehead (left)

A punky, very blonde look cut extremely short at the sides to emphasise the fullness on top. An ideal easy-care style for very fine hair to scrunch dry or spike dry with the fingers and hair gel. It will need regular trimming (right)

Here a curly perm is combined with an interesting cut to give a delicate Edwardian look to short hair. A fragile hairstyle that softens heavy features (below)

HAIR BY VERNON FOR VIDAL SASSOON

HAIR: TONY RIZZO AT SANRIZZ

Long Afro plaits tied with ribbons and beads create an ethnic look for black hair that's suitable for all occasions — and the decoration can be altered to suit your mood. The style takes time to achieve, but once you've plaited it, you can leave it until it next wants washing (below)

A sultry and elegant look that shows off the model's top-condition hair. Height on top and the falling fringe of glossy ringlets complement a delicately shaped face and a neatly pointed chin (right)

A very dramatic look — almost two hairstyles in one. The top hair has been halo-cut and allowed its natural frizz, while the back has been straightened and cut into a formalised mane. Fun colours have been sprayed onto the hair for a jungle effect (above)

A classic oriental look with a full severe fringe shows off the model's beautiful straight and heavy hair. The geometrical effect is continued with the centre parting and the jaunty behind-the-ears cut to underline the delicacy of the model's bone structure and her long uptilted eyes, dramatised by kohl eyeliner (right)

An oriental look with a difference. A lock of hair fanning out from the crown has been tinted red, for a dressy effect, while a tuft of very short hair at the crown creates the illusion of long hair secured with chopsticks. The hair is cut neatly over the ears and into the nape of the neck (below)

A very glamourous 40s look for permanently waved mid-length hair. The hair is styled with rollers and traditional setting lotion to achieve the formal rippling waves made so popular by screen goddesses such as Lauren Bacall (left)

Puckish and sopisticated, this highly original style is based on the artfully simple French pleat. The serpentine wriggles around the forehead and behind the ear need a roller, setting gel, and plenty of patience. A shorter wriggle falling forward onto the face — or several shorter wriggles — would last longer (below)

HAIR BY THOMAS AT NEVILLE DANIEL

Oriental elegance. For this style you need plenty of long thick hair. Piled on top of the head in two great waves, and slithering over the shoulder from behind, it creates the impression of cool inscrutability (left)

HAIR BY BRUCE HUNTER FOR WELLA

A perfect cut for shoulder-length hair. Set on large rollers and then brushed back and away from the face, this is a look that needs careful attention for formal occasions (right)

HAIR: SHERMAN PERU

This style harks back to the 50s, when bouffants teamed with ponytails were all the rage. But there is no mistaking today's softer look, with the emphasis on the condition of the hair, and the use of hair gel eliminates the need for too much harmful backbrushing (above)

This exotic look is emphasised by blond highlighting. The short front hair is curled to give height to a low forehead and the rest of the hair is sleeked back into a classic French roll. The one loose curl at its base softens a potentially severe look. A style that's neat, easy to achieve and stays looking smooth all day (below)

Fine hair has been given a deep-conditioning treatment, wet-set on small rollers and dressed into this stunning style. Firm but gentle setting lotion and hairspray give both body and hold. A very elegant look for medium-long hair on formal occasions (right)

A classic backswept look for thick, medium-long hair. The model's natural curl has been tamed with heated rollers and the subtle highlights accentuate the bouyant movement of the hair (above)

A sleek and ultra-sophisticated look for evening on long fine hair. Highlights follow the soft movement up and over the head. The gently falling fringe and tendrils around the ears and nape add a carefree air to a style that might otherwise be too formal (right)

A youthful and exuberant look is achieved on medium-long hair with a soft perm. The hair has been wet-set and the front turned over and pinned back so that one single curl escapes and tumbles over the forehead (left)

HAIR: CLAIROL

This parallel bob on thick straight hair has fine highlights through the front to give a delicate tone and a look of elegance (left)

Thick, medium-long hair is upswept with a ragged fringe and a complementary ragged topknot — the tails at the nape echo the fringed effect (top right)

This hair has been superbly cut into an asymmetric bob. Its length gives the model flexibility — she can wear it up or down, back, forward, flat or full, as in the photograph. Her make-up is soft and subtle for day wear — for evenings she can add more colour and definition (bottom right)

An easy style for thick, medium-length hair. The full, heavy fringe draws attention to the model's almond eyes. The ends of the hair are flicked up slightly in blow drying (below)

This dramatic look is achieved by roller-setting medium-long hair. The top hair is brushed up and secured in the middle of the head, while the side hair is secured on the crown. The back hair is left to flow free. The style shows off the wonderful conditions of the model's hair

The hair has been graduated at the sides and square cut. The back of the hair has been cut into the shape of a bob and the top left spiky (top right)

The hair has been cut with strong graduation through the sides, following through to the nape of the neck, and layered in. The top of the hair is graduated on the round and the front sliced — the scissors are left open and pulled gently through the front of the hair to give a more striking effect (top left)

The hair has been cut up towards the temples and short through the sides, following through into the back hairline. It is cut very short underneath (right)

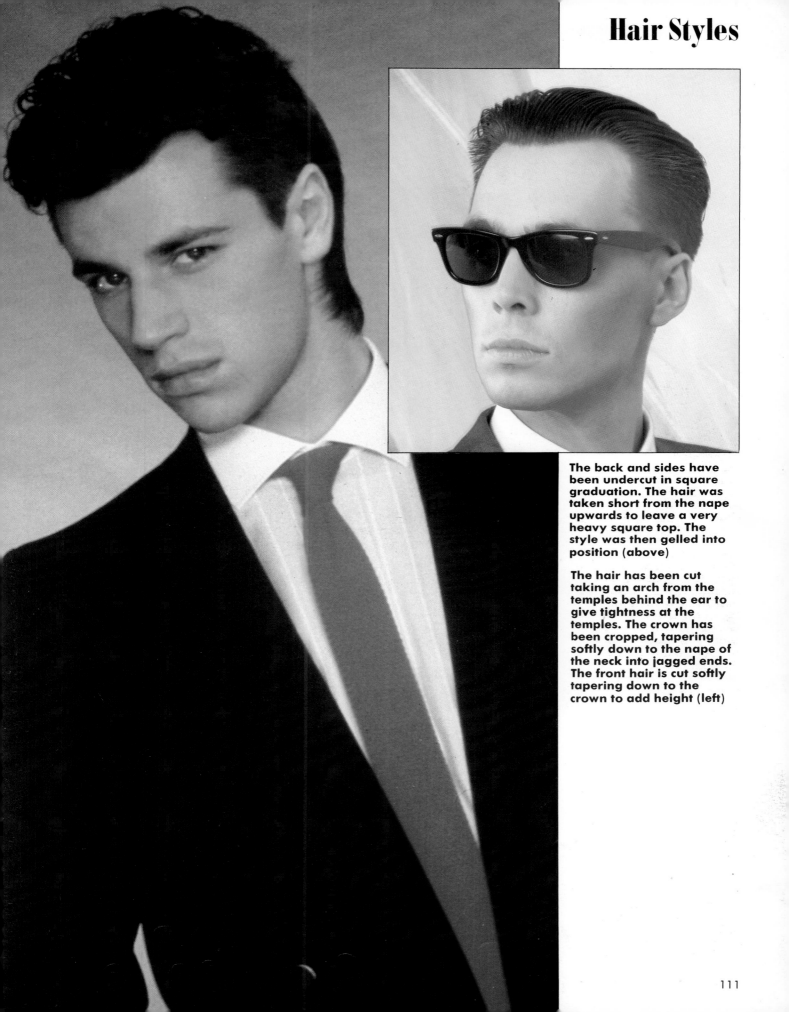

The back and sides have been undercut in square graduation. The hair was taken short from the nape upwards to leave a very heavy square top. The style was then gelled into position (above)

The hair has been cut taking an arch from the temples behind the ear to give tightness at the temples. The crown has been cropped, tapering softly down to the nape of the neck into jagged ends. The front hair is cut softly tapering down to the crown to add height (left)

Hair that doesn't fall into the eyes or lose its shape when splashed is ideal for watersports. To make sense of a straggly hairline, the underneath is cut shorter. This gives volume and character to the larger, graduated shape on the sides and back. A step of weight has also been cut into the back to give the face more focus (**right**)

This is a style that looks good in action because the hair has been undercut -- the underneath hair is cut shorter and the top hair is left longer to overlap it. The lower hair has been coloured darker and the crown highlighted to emphasise the swinging movement of the cut (far (left)

The hair has been undercut at the sides and is blended with heavy graduation into a bob at the back. The effect is to create a wing-like movement, with the sides spilling into the breezy back (left)

This is an easy-to-manage blunt cut. The hair is blown upwards with a brush to give movement, but it can also be dried naturally for a spiky, textured look of the same shape. The heavily graduated undercut short sides and blunt short back give a crispness to relaxed hair (bottom left)

This haircut looks free and moves well, but it has been cut using very precise and controlled techniques. The hair has been heavily graduated through the sides to give maximum width to hair of any texture (right)

A neat, small head shape with a sculptured feel. The hair has been cut short at the back and sides and scissor-overcombed at the back with longer graduations on the top. It is cropped close to the sideburns to blend into the sides of the hair (below)

As the model's hair is Afro, it is first slightly relaxed to give a wavy look. It is then cut short all over, with the hairline in a 'W' shape at the nape. Styling gel has been applied to encourage the waves

The hair has been lightly permed on top and coloured a warm brown. Gel is applied while the hair is wet for a wet look and the sides are left smooth and flat

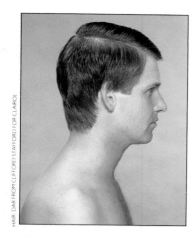

This boy-next-door haircut is a little behind the times — the model wanted a style that would allow him to look well groomed and fairly conservative as well as fashionable

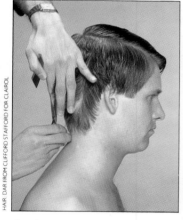

The hair was styled in sections from the ear to the eyebrow and lifted 1 cm ($\frac{1}{2}$ inch) from the face before cutting. The front was cut in an asymmetric line, the hair pulled right up and back toward the crown in order to give a heavy fringe

The finished look, brushed upwards, is smart and up-to-date. It can be combed down and back for a more conservative short-back-and-sides look, still very much a style of today

This wonderfully soft ponytail is an unusual creation on jaw-length hair tinted a warm harvest gold. The front and top hair is looped into wayward curls and fastened in the middle of the head with a daisy. The back hair is brushed down smoothly to curl behind the ears (right)

Afro hair always looks delightful in an off-the-centre top knot — this style boasts two that balance each other perfectly, and a soft fringe. Decorate the top knots with flowers for a romantic look (below)

Another special look for mid-length hair — this time the back hair has been brushed up softly and secured at the crown, while the top hair revels in a froth of loose curls that end in soft tendrils at brow level, enhancing superbly made-up eyes (above)

HAIR BY RANJIT AT CRIMPERS FOR L'ORÉAL

A curly perm gives life and texture to thick mid-length hair that otherwise hangs in an uninteresting flat curtain. The square cut, with fullness both on the top of the head and at the shoulder line, shortens a long narrow face (left)

A mass of tight curls — effervescent on top and behind — are smoothed back at the sides to slim the face and secured with a slide. The top curls are teased out until they are light and wispy and the main body of the hair is left in glossy corkscrew tendrils (below)

Curly hair swept sleekly to the side and slicked down with oil mousse looks lusciously tropical against a brown skin. A sari-style dress enhances the exotic flavour (below)

HAIR BY KENSI AT TONI & GUY

HAIR BY AVRAM FOR VIDAL SASSOON

HAIR BY ROBERT FIELDING

HAIR: ALEC FOR VIDAL SASSOON

The model's soft curly hair is rather dense and heavy for her delicate features (above)

With her hair cropped above her ears in a soft fluffy style, the model's waif-like features and her large dark eyes are beautifully accentuated. The style is achieved with a mousse and the curls are teased out with the fingers as the hair dries (right)

HAIR: VIDAL SASSOON

HAIR: DANIEL GALVIN

This long pre-Raphaelite look, swept dramatically over to one side, has been deep-conditioned to protect it from sun, salt and sand. It is particularly important to condition treated hair before going on holiday

Long, lightly permed hair has been scrunch dried with hair gel to create this dramatic tinselly look. The movement of the hair is accentuated with highlights (right)

The model is making the most of her naturally curly hair. Tendrils of tiny corkscrew curls are teased out from under the bandeau that holds the rest of the hair in place (below)

LONG HAIR

A ponytail keeps your hair out of your face and stops it blowing into unsightly tangles out of doors. But don't feel you must always secure the tail at the back of your head. Try it in a cascade on the top or side of your head like this model, and fasten it in position with a striking slide. (right)

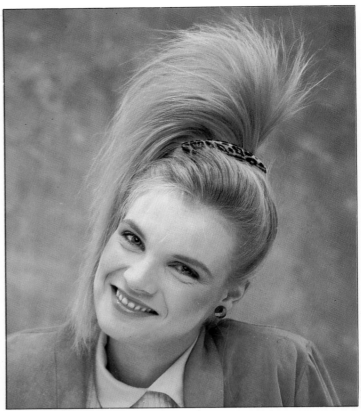

If you have a low forehead, it's always a good idea to dress long hair up, to give your face extra height. This smooth, sophisticated and rather Spanish-looking style is achieved with styling gel and heated rollers. As the model's hair is heavy, only a minimum of backbrushing was needed. The ponytail prevents the style from becoming too severe (above)

A soft elegant style that presents a comfortable compromise between wearing your hair up or down. The hair is swept up from the ears, twisted over and secured in the middle of the head creating a heart shape, which emphasises the model's delicate heart-shaped face

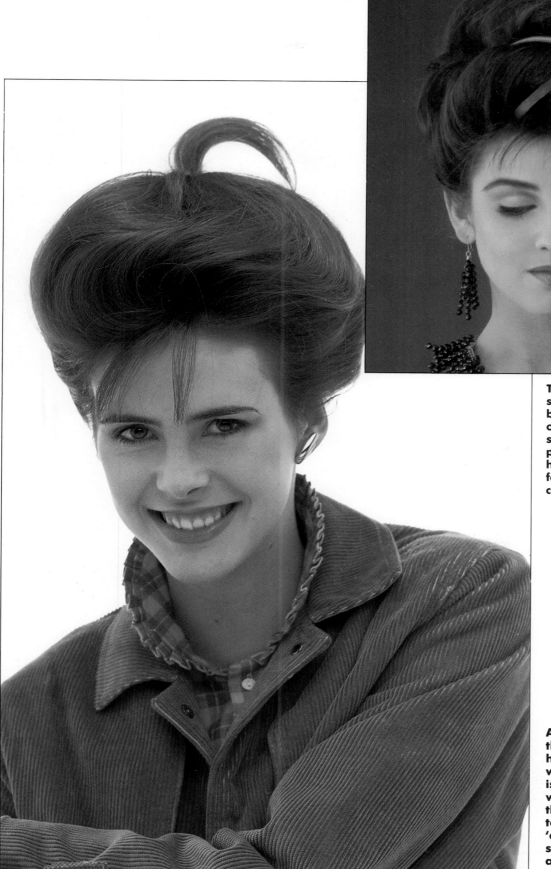

The model's thick hair is set on large rollers, brushed out and sectioned off with ribbons, then secured in a full, loose pony tail on top of her head. The tail is brushed forward in a cascade of curl (above)

A casual topknot shows off the model's soft heavy hair, which is tinted a warm rich brown. The hair is wet-set on large rollers with setting lotion. It is then brushed up and back to create a swirling 'cottage loaf' effect, and secured at the crown with a perky tail of hair acting as a tassel on top (left)

Hair extensions — bobtails, ragtails and locks — are a revolutionary new way of altering your hair length. This style transforms fine hair into a thick mass of long romantic ringlets

An Afro-plaited look with extensions to match your colour and texture. The style can be left through shampooing as long as rinsing is thorough (below)

A really dramatic look that makes Medusa-like tails out of medium-length hair. Acrylic extensions can be woven in to hair that is about 7 cm (3-4 inches) long to make the hair any length you wish (left)

Here Afro plaits are woven into European hair and dressed high in an elaborate ponytail for a wide-eyed filmstar look

Longish blonde hair is swept in to a French pleat that hides the join, securing a long thick ponytail of false hair. An unforgettable evening style (right)

This style with waist-long extensions on short blonde hair takes time to achieve, but the results are spectacular and well worth the effort for a special occasion (below)

HAIR: RONNIE AT ANTENNA

HAIR: DEBBIE DANNELL AT ANTENNA

A dramatic Hiawatha look makes a stunning evening appearance against a plunging plain black gown. Silken tassels are braided into upswept blond hair — strongly made-up eyes and lips complete a theatrical appearance (left)

A fantasy wedding headdress — or pure fancy dress. The model's hair was roller-set and fluffed out into curls on top of her head. The tassels were cleverly fixed on in an imitation of a Regency look (below)

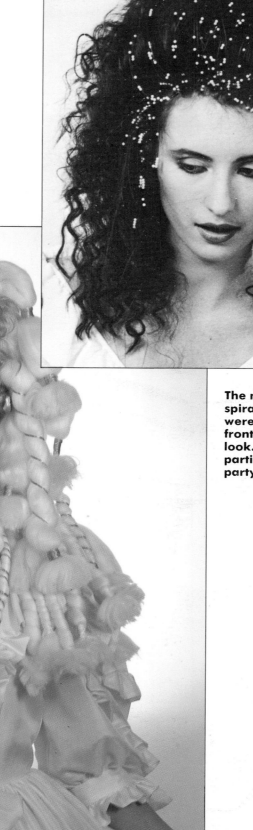

The model's hair was spiral-set and tiny pearls were threaded into the front hair for a romantic look. This style is particularly suitable for a party or wedding (above)

HAIR MAXINE AT PIERRE ALEXANDRE

HAIR MAXINE AT PIERRE ALEXANDRE

Index